Red Mill

Red Mill

It's Not How You Start,
It's How You Finish

Murray Schwartz
with
Michael Levin

Publishing by Redwood Publishing
Orange County, California
www.redwooddigitalpublishing.com

Printed in the United States of America

First Printing, 2020

ISBN: 978-1-952106-23-1 (hardcover)
ISBN: 978-1-952106-24-8 (paperback)
ISBN: 978-1-952106-25-5 (e-book)

Library of Congress Number: 2020903899

Disclaimer: I have tried to recreate events, locales and conversations from my memories of them. I have made every effort to ensure that the information in this book was correct at press time, the author and publisher do not assume and hereby disclaim any liability to any party for any loss, damage, or disruption caused by errors or omissions, whether such errors or omissions result from negligence, accident, or any other cause.

Cover Illustration by Yarikart
Book design and production by Ghislain Viau

Contents

Introduction

I was an innocent. I don't think anyone ever saw that. How could any of us see clearly in a business that's all about surfaces? Eventually, however, I saw most things more clearly than I did the day I walked into the William Morris Agency, a guileless kid from the Bronx.

When I started with George Wood, I didn't know there were finer things out there. I'd glimpsed them, but I didn't know they could become mine. George changed everything, though. After working with him for a few years, I would rise through the ranks at the agency and go on to build and run the multimedia empire Merv Griffin Enterprises.

The first time I saw George, I was a mailroom boy at the William Morris Agency in New York. It was the 1950s and I was a kid, still in my teens, delivering mail to the guys who ran the careers of the most important entertainers in the world: names like Frank Sinatra, Sammy Davis Jr., and Marilyn Monroe.

I carried the mail in an army-green box slung across my new suit. Inside the mailbox was an accordion file, each section labeled with the names of the agents: Jordan, Lefkowitz, Leon, Weiss, Wolfson, Wood, and so on. The bag was heavy, and as I passed the agents working their magic in their sleek, modern offices, I felt the gulf between us. How did those guys leap over that chasm to get where they were? How could I do the same?

George Wood seemed even more remote than all the others—a star several light-years away. Yet he shone the brightest, leading me to believe he was not just any star, but the sun.

That was certainly how it seemed. I remember the first time I passed him in the hallway, burdened by my mailbag, my suit jacket bunched up under the strap. He looked grand, style oozing from every pore. George wasn't tall, but he looked it in a vicuña overcoat and brown suede hat tipped to the side, with a single gold-and-brown feather arching out of the hatband. He wore alligator shoes that shone as brightly as the chrome bumpers on a new 1953 Cadillac. I'd never seen alligator shoes before. I wanted to meet him. I wanted to know him. I wanted to *be* him.

But as George made his way down the hall, I noticed that he had a strange walk. He tossed his weight from one foot to another in an awkward limp, as if he was trying to steady himself on a rolling ship. For all his expensive clothes, I could see from the start that George was not without flaws.

I watched that walk for a full year, delivering mail to the agents at William Morris. I continued to ponder that question: *How could I get where they were?* But nothing was happening. I knew I had to take things into my own hands—something had to change.

I delivered mail to George Wood's office, just as I did for all the other agents. You weren't supposed to go *into* their offices, however. You just were supposed to leave the mail with the secretary who guarded every agent's kingdom. But one fateful day, George's secretary wasn't there.

I figured I had nothing to lose. Without hesitation, I grabbed George's bundle of mail from my bag and walked past the secretary's desk, through George's door, and right up to him. He was sitting back in his chair, his feet up on the desk, reading the paper. There were the alligator shoes, gleaming in the light. He was dressed as usual in an expensive, custom-made blue suit and a monogrammed shirt with French cuffs. George *always* wore French cuffs. As I placed the mail on his desk, George lowered his newspaper and looked at me, cockeyed. I would come to know this confrontational stare well. "What the fuck are you doing?" he said.

"I'm delivering the mail," I said, as casually as I could muster.

"You're not supposed to put it in here. It goes outside."

"I really wanted to meet you, Mr. Wood," I said. "I'm not getting ahead. Things aren't working out for me in the mailroom."

"How long have you been here?"

"A year," I told him.

He looked me over. "What are you doing tonight?" he asked.

"No plans."

"Meet me at Elmo's," he said.

I was stunned. Just like that, George Wood had invited me out with him for the evening.

I nodded and strode out the door, trying to look as confident as I had when I'd entered. And in a moment, the confidence I was faking turned real . . . and rapidly transformed to cockiness. This was going to be easy. First, though, I'd have to find Elmo's, whatever that was.

I asked around the mailroom. "Elmo's" stood for El Morocco, the most glamorous nightclub in New York at that time, which meant it was probably the most glamorous place in the world.

That evening, I went home to the Bronx to put on my finery: a plaid jacket with wide lapels and a tie with a clip that read "10%." I'd had it made for me at a place called Tie City, and it was my talisman for success. Once dressed, I got back on the subway, taking it down to El Morocco on East 54th Street between Lexington and Third Avenue. When I got there, John, the maître d', showed me to "Mr. Wood's table." Feeling very cool, I sat down. George was surrounded by a group of beautiful women and crisply groomed men.

He looked at me and said, "Is the circus in town?" He pronounced circus, "soy-kuss."

"I don't know," I said. "I'll check. Why?" Maybe he wanted me to book it.

But before I could fully envision the promotion I'd get from bringing the circus to town, he replied, "Because you're dressed like a fuckin' clown."

And with that, he jammed some dough into my jacket pocket and told me to get lost. I think it was a hundred dollars, which was a lot of money to me—worth about ten times as much as it would be today. I was too surprised to respond.

Nowadays, if a kid experienced the same kind of treatment, he'd probably get a lawyer and sue both George and the agency for creating a hostile work environment. But it was a different time. Back then, no lawyer would've taken that case, and I certainly wouldn't have thought to get one (nor would I have been able to afford the hourly rate). I didn't really have any option other than to leave, and to try to conceal my embarrassment as I made my way out.

I stood on the sidewalk on 54th Street for maybe a second or two. I've never been one to get too emotional. I just figure out what needs to be done, and what needed to be done was to keep George's attention. Here was a chance to get out of the mailroom and into something else, something better, though I didn't know what that would be. I wasn't about to squander it.

I started walking, trying to figure out what to do. I was heated, moving quickly, and before I knew it I was in Times Square. I looked up. Bond Clothiers stood directly in front of me. Bond was a famous men's store dating back to 1914. It was known for its two-trouser suits. The joke at the time was, "With my luck, I burned a hole in the jacket."

The Bond storefront was massive, spanning a city block. The Times Square branch opened in 1940 and was known as the "Cathedral of Clothing." No kidding. Two statues, thirty feet tall, topped the building. The neon sign rose three stories high, dwarfing the cars and people below: B-O-N-D. At the center of the "O" was an enormous clock. Bond seemed not only to sit at the crossroads of the world; it felt like it *was* the crossroads.

Across Times Square on the Broadway side was the famous Camel billboard. I could see the giant blue smoke rings blown by the cardboard face of an archetypal mid-century American male—a business type, straight out of *The Man in the Gray Flannel Suit*. Those rings cascaded over the evening traffic. They puffed out of a large, round hole in the American Man's mouth, giving him a look of surprised pleasure.

On the mannequin in the front window was a snappy blue suit, just like Mr. Wood's. A sign advertised that it came with two pairs of pants, as was the Bond way. There it was in the window: my new life, just sitting there on a dummy. I stepped inside.

"I want that suit," I told the first salesman I saw, pointing to the window.

"Sure, kid. We can have it ready for you in a few days."

I said, "No. I want it *now*." I pulled the wad of cash from my jacket pocket and handed it to the guy.

He looked at the money and shrugged. "OK," he said. "We'll get it for you *now*." I guess a hundred dollars was a lot of money to him, too.

When the suit was ready, I took off what had been my most impressive set of clothing just an hour earlier and threw it away in the store's trash can.

Dressed for the second time that evening, I emerged on the streets of New York with a new look and new identity and walked nine blocks uptown, six-and-a-half crosstown, until I was back at El Morocco. When I got there, I trotted right past the maître d'. I knew where I was heading. George and his glamorous set were still at their big table, drinking and laughing. Silently, I took my seat.

"Where'd you get the suit?" George asked. I told him what I'd done, how I'd bought a new suit at Bond and made the salesman tailor it on the spot. George's expression changed. A moment later he said, "Tomorrow morning, you'll be my new secretary."

I nodded, trying to conceal my joy. What a leap! It was like jumping the Grand Canyon. To work for George, the dealmaker behind Sammy Davis Jr., Frank Sinatra, and the whole Rat Pack, was a dream I didn't know one *could* dream.

In hindsight, it was my destiny. George's world was hypnotic, dazzling. A year earlier I hadn't known such a world existed. There was just a blurry notion of "better." And now, here it was. "Better" had fallen into my lap. Maybe it wasn't an accident after all that I'd found it so easy to walk into George Wood's office.

Some people don't believe in luck, but it's actually everywhere. Look at Brad Pitt and Angelina Jolie. They didn't do anything to look like that. Look at Prince George of England. All he had to do was get born. That's true for all of us, even if we aren't born into beauty or money. None of us ask to arrive on Earth, but it really is the chance of a lifetime. Then it's up to us to find our own luck, to make something of ourselves. Meeting George was that luck for me. Whatever George Wood meant to me, whatever he gave me, I've never lost it. The effect that man had on me was a drug.

But before I could meet him and become a person I dared not dream I'd be, I had to make it out of the Bronx, where I'd been born and raised.

CHAPTER 1

The Wall of Flowers

The Red Mill—the namesake of Paris's Moulin Rouge, a land-mark with similar theatrical offerings—sat under the "El," the elevated train that ran along Jerome Avenue in the Bronx. Jerome Avenue is still there, but the Red Mill stopped spinning its sails some time ago. It lives on in my memory, where it always feels like Saturday night inside, and the stripper's agent, Moe Gold, is flashing his bankroll, a Cuban cigar clenched between his teeth, while a beautiful dancer dashes from her dressing room to the stage, her costume shimmering under the spotlights.

My father worked at the Red Mill as a jack-of-all-trades, taking care of a range of chores. At the club, my father was "Schwartzy," a nickname I hated. I was "Sonny," Schwartzy's kid, and after school I'd go to the Red Mill with my books and homework, and I, too, would become a jack-of-all-trades. The Red Mill was a kind of Eden, far preferable to our family apartment, 1697 Andrews Avenue #4K, a cramped fourth-floor walk-up, also in the Bronx.

At the Red Mill, I had my run of the place. I could make french fries for my friends, Joey, Gary, and Paul, and give them Cokes with as many maraschino cherries as I could fit in the glass. They loved to come down after school, hang out with me, and see the first show. Who could blame them? It was such a treat.

Of course, we played outside too—stickball on the streets of the Bronx. It was a street version of baseball, but scrappier, where the winner was determined by who could hit a Spalding ball the distance between the manhole covers that ran down the middle of the road (four covers was an automatic home run). But there was simply no comparison to an afternoon spent in the hazy glow of the Red Mill.

We didn't get a lot of daylight under the El, and anyway, the sun rose at night inside the Red Mill. The house band was its birdsong, and manhattans and brandy sidecars were its morning dew. There was a clock in the center of the mill's sails. It never worked, but it was right twice a day.

People find it hard to believe now, but far from ruining or corrupting me, my boyhood in that neighborhood strip club, and my father's strong presence in it, taught me all kinds of lessons—integrity included. I just didn't know where those lessons would lead me; as it turned out, they took me pretty far. But we'll get there.

In those days, the Bronx was a world unto itself. I lived in a roughed-up area filled with elegant street names—University Avenue, Sedgwick Avenue, Nelson Avenue, each of which had its own gang. But the Red Mill was no dive; it was an upscale place—not seedy at all. It had grandeur, a flash of spectacle that attracted people like moths. I don't remember any fighting, or ever hearing anything about drugs. Gambling, yes—there was lots of it: numbers, horses, baseball games, you name it; bookmakers were regulars at the bar. But for the most part, it was harmless, a victimless crime. Just people living their lives, betting a few dollars on a horse or a game.

Plenty of cops were there too, taking in the scenery and putting the kibosh on any problems that would come up. In exchange for helping keep the place in order, they got free meals—and probably a cut of the bookmakers' profits.

The patrons were elegant. They were mostly couples—men who looked like they'd stepped right off the big screen, and ladies who wore little hats, their hair in neat waves, tapping their long cigarettes against the edges of the ashtrays that were on every table. One picture I have from back in the day features two dapper gentlemen, dressed in suits and bright ties, the ladies by their sides in those little hats and long gloves. On the table in front of them is a lavish meal laid out just so, with cocktails and glasses of wine, huge steaks, and fresh fruit. The Red Mill was a destination for people looking for some fun and enchantment—magic, even—in the wilds of the Bronx.

And it wasn't just strippers those patrons came to see; it was a whole show. First the band would take the stage and play a number, typically followed by some stand-up comedy—top names would test their material at the Red Mill before bringing their acts to bigger venues. (The actor and comedian Al Nesor was a frequent guest.) A singer would come next . . . and then it was the strippers who'd close out the show.

A group of six would perform—all in matching costumes, five of them serving as backup dancers to the loveliest one. The girls looked like the most popular burlesque dancers of the day—Blaze Starr or Tempest Storm or Lili St. Cyr—all of whom were incredibly hot, though perhaps more glamorous than pretty.

The Fourth of July at the Red Mill was a big event. We'd stay up until the wee hours of the morning the night before, inflating red, white, and blue balloons and rigging them up with nets so they'd fall at just the right moment. We decorated the tables with little American flags. The show on the Fourth was a true act of patriotism. While our bandleader and star trumpeter, Joe Duro, played marches by John Philip Sousa, such as "Stars and Stripes Forever," the strippers twirled their tassels. After World War II, the song "The US Air Force" was also hugely popular: "*Off we go, into the wild blue yonder . . . .*" Joe played that one too, and as the song reached its crescendo, the strippers' tassels became propellers, spinning with perfect precision.

Then the balloons dropped down from the ceiling, bouncing across the tables, and the patrons would tap them lightly toward one another with their fingertips, enchanted by the scene unfolding in front of them. *This is show business*, I remember thinking. That it was—show business with a hint of sex, unlike the displays most strip clubs put on today.

There was a certain innocence to it all. For instance, while you could look, you certainly couldn't touch. The girls made tips, but you wouldn't dare slip bills into the waistbands of their bikinis. In fact, my father was charged with enforcing that policy. He had a shillelagh, a thick wooden club that served as a deterrent to any customer who might get ideas about crossing the invisible line between his table and the stage. In my favorite photo of my dad, he's standing behind the bar, shillelagh in hand, ready to do what was necessary to maintain order.

There was a famous story about a guy who tried to grab one of the strippers. My father, the keeper of the shillelagh, brought it down on the guy's knuckles, smashing them hard. The strippers and waitresses were always safe. The customers got the message, some the hard way. But once they knew the rules and obeyed them, they were always welcome—and that guy in particular kept coming back. Hey, a customer is a customer. Plus, we never needed to call the cops, since they were already there for the show.

The mores of the times also protected the dignity of the women. If they had any activities outside of their assigned duties, it was up to them; no one encouraged it. It wasn't made public. There was that sense of innocence again. Or maybe it was privacy. Or both. That stayed with me—so much so that a woman I recently dated told me she found the way I treated women—with dignity and respect—fascinating. She thinks I probably learned it in the Red Mill.

I agree. If I learned anything, it was to be charming and pleasant—never creepy or crude. Over the years, I've found that charm goes a long way. At five foot seven, I'm certainly not winning them over with my height.

And what of the strippers' physiques? They were more Rubenesque than the women you might find in a gentleman's club today, with big, natural breasts. I don't know if that was a prerequisite for the job, or if women just had larger breasts in that era, but I never saw make-believe—or perhaps I should say *enhanced*—breasts until I was older.

The strippers were fun too. In fact, my mom would hang out with them. She'd visit the Red Mill, and they would all sit around and schmooze. Off duty and outside of the club, they just looked like nice gals. I remember one of them coming over to the house just to visit. I barely recognized her without the tassels.

While many of them were a little older, in their forties—which was pretty old back then—none of them appeared to be librarians, at least not the way librarians looked during that era: old and grizzled, with purple varicose veins peeking through their hose. They all looked like they wanted to be Hollywood movie stars. And to me, the vibe of the Red Mill was just as glamorous as any Hollywood club.

Of course, this bit of glamour also included characters with names like "Sam the Pee-House Man," who presided over the men's room. He would pour ice cubes into the bottom of the urinal (for what reason, I'm not sure). But some places—like the 21 Club in Manhattan—still do that today.

Sam would always set up a little table in the men's room. On top of a white tablecloth, he'd place a dish of peppermints, a brush, aftershave—Old Spice, of course—and a bottle of Listerine. He'd be there to hand out towels too. I'd help him, watering down the mouthwash (why spend all that money on pure Listerine?) and filling the dish with those mints, the kind with the red and white swirls. Sam would tip me for my efforts.

Above Sam's table was a framed poster that read, "As you go through life, brother, whatever be your goal, keep your eye upon the doughnut and not upon the hole." Wise words that are still important today.

Sam's wife, "Mrs. Sam," attended to the women's room. Sam and his wife were African American, and more elegant to me than any of the other people who worked there—stylish and reserved, always dressed in very clean, crisp, white uniforms, whereas many of the other staff just looked like they were working in a bar. They'd been there for as long as I could remember.

At the Red Mill, everyone had nicknames. We weren't terribly advanced at the time, and we called the Chinese chef "Fong," never asking his real name. He was a great cook, always making what the people wanted. He was known for his succulent roast chicken.

There was Dutch the bartender/bouncer, a tall ex-Marine in a vest. He looked like Sterling Hayden, who played Capt. McCluskey, the cop who got shot in *The Godfather*. Dutch dated the strippers and hit on every woman who walked through the door, even if she came with a date. He was quite the character.

The bandleader, Joe Duro, was a poor man's Ray Anthony. Everyone thought he was the classiest guy. He had an air of mystery about him. Then, one day, he jumped off a building in Washington Heights, and just like that, there was no more Joe Duro. His death shocked everyone at the Red Mill, including me.

The owners were Nat Kaye and his wife. Nat was big and fat, and Mrs. Kaye had the heaviest New York Jewish accent I'd ever heard—on nights when resident comic Al Nesor took the stage, Mrs. Kaye would say, "Appearing tonight is *Hal Nessna*." She never corrected her mistake, and after a while, it stuck.

I'm not saying we were sophisticates, but we weren't without royalty.

Nat had three brothers, Herman, Charlie, and Leon. Charlie was his partner in the business, and Leon owned a liquor store nearby. That store's biggest account was the Red Mill. Later, when I got older, I always felt there was something fishy going on. I'm not sure if they were breaking the law in any way—although it probably wouldn't have mattered, as the cops were some of our best customers—but Nat and his brothers certainly weren't what I'd call pillars of society.

In movies, it was always the tough guys and mobsters who owned the nightclubs, and I imagined the Kaye family operated in a similar manner. Leon seemed to be the sophisticated one of the four. I was always envious of Leon's son, who got to have his bar mitzvah at the Red Mill. The ceremony was certainly a break from business as usual.

At bar mitzvahs today they sometimes serve lobster, but back then they at least *tried* to stick to tradition. The Kayes bought kosher food—chopped liver and corned beef—to be prepared by the Chinese chef, but so what? A corned beef is a corned beef, right?

They closed the curtains around the bandstand and brought in an accordion player to play the Jewish standards—"Hava Nagila" and the like. Leon's son made his bar mitzvah speech on the stage where the strippers would normally be twirling tassels, but with those curtains closed, it looked like any bar mitzvah you'd see in a catering hall. It was the kind of event any average Jewish family in the Bronx would have been proud to host, albeit held in a burlesque nightclub.

I wasn't granted the same opportunity. We'd hoped to hold the party at the Red Mill when the time came for my own bar mitzvah, but the owners wouldn't allow it. Instead, we shoved extra chairs into the living room of our tiny apartment and everyone crammed in awkwardly. My father spent the whole night before cooking: home-made corned beef, pastrami, and potato salad. It was humiliating. Everyone knew it was humiliating, but it was what we had. I remember thinking it would never end. All I wanted to do was run out of there and go hit a couple of balls against the concrete wall of a building.

While the celebration was a dismal affair, my bar mitzvah gift was nothing short of miraculous. It was nothing like anything any of my pals at Hebrew school received—not even close. Later that night, after the guests had filed out, my father said, "OK, kid. Change your clothes. You're coming with me."

"Where to?" I asked.

"We're going to the Red Mill."

I was surprised. I rarely went to the Red Mill on a Saturday night. And it had been my bar mitzvah, so I assumed I'd just stay home, then maybe go out later with my buddies and get into some harmless mischief. We liked to sneak into Yankee Stadium or just walk through the neighborhood, flirting with the girls we'd run into or stopping for a soda and fries.

"Hurry up," my father said as we walked through the dark, the August air hot and thick with humidity. He was walking so quickly that I practically had to run to keep up with him.

We arrived just before showtime. The girls were all dressed up. The bartenders were furiously pouring drinks. The smell of perfume and cigarettes permeated the air.

One girl in particular seemed to be waiting for us. She was beautiful and sweet, more petite than the others, and probably a bit younger as well. Dressed in her costume for the night, she looked like a precious jewel. My father said to her, "Take care of Sonny."

"OK," she said. With that, he walked away. We stood there, in the hallway outside of the dressing rooms. She winked at me.

It was only then that I caught on. My father took the idea of manhood seriously, and his gift to me was to arrange for one of the strippers at the Red Mill to give me a proper initiation: a blow job.

That's right, a blow job.

You may be horrified, but it was a different era. And to put it in context, given the neighborhood in which we lived, my dad knew I'd most likely have my first sexual experiences in places—and with people—that were far from safe, and certainly not friendly. Venereal disease was common. Getting crabs was considered the best-case scenario. Who knew who was out there?

Around that time, the guys I knew would rent either the back of a house or a garage so we could hang out. There was a girl we'd invite over. Her name was Sandy, and everyone would take turns with her. My father was concerned about that, so he decided that an initiation within the walls of the Red Mill was probably for the best.

I was terrified—and overwhelmingly excited.

There was a bare light bulb overhead, and I fixed my gaze on it as she unzipped my fly, got on her knees, and put me in her mouth right there in the hallway. Anyone could have come by, but no one did.

It was my first time, and I didn't know what to expect. The experience was erotic but strange. I thought I felt my eyeballs fall out, but I could still see the light overhead. And though it probably only lasted a few minutes, time seemed to slow while I stared at that bulb. Though I don't recall the woman's name, it was a moment I'd remember for the rest of my life.

"Did you have fun?" my dad asked afterward.

I'd always been a shy, polite kid—always respectful. "Yes," I said, feeling my cheeks flush with embarrassment. I mumbled my thanks for the gift.

Today, most kids get pens or watches, or maybe some government bonds. But in those days, what my dad did for me wasn't that unusual. Was it a strange rationale? Yes. Was he trying to protect me? Yes. Was it the right thing to do? My father didn't always know what the right thing to do was. But I'm sure Leon's son—and anyone lucky enough to be the son of someone who worked there—got the same gift. And trust me, it was better than a fountain pen.

The fact that the Kayes weren't interested in lending us the Red Mill for my bar mitzvah didn't mean they ruled out private events altogether. As long as clients could pay for the privilege, they were willing to rent the place out. One day, my dad was assigned the job of getting the Red Mill ready for a wedding. There would be booze at the reception—a big moneymaker—and the potential to pull in extra cash was too tempting for the Kayes to pass up.

So the club was closed down for a day to get the place ready. My father was very creative, and though he never had much of a chance to develop his gift, he shined when given an opportunity like this one. He wanted to impress the couple and do things right, and that meant he would need an extra set of hands. So he recruited me to help decorate for the wedding. Of course, I did what my father told me to do.

I had no idea what it meant to decorate the Red Mill for that kind of celebration, and I'm not sure my father did either, but we set out to transform it into a place fit to host someone's grandmother.

The day before the wedding, the two of us headed down to the flower district on Eighth Avenue in the Thirties in Manhattan. The florists in the flower district made lush, extravagant bouquets for high-end events at venues across the city, but in doing so, a lot of flowers were broken. The imperfect blooms couldn't be used for bouquets, so the flower merchants sold them at a heavy discount.

My father and I bought hundreds of discarded flowers, gathering them into big bags. On the way home, I was nearly overcome by the scent of so many different kinds of blooms. By the time we got back to the Red Mill, it was early evening. A few of my buddies came over, hoping to get time with the strippers. They were disappointed when it turned out the strippers weren't there, but they helped nonetheless. We hung large white tablecloths in front of the bandstand, creating a bare canvas, and began stapling the flowers to them. Roses, tulips, peonies, and lilies, plus hundreds of white, pink, and red carnations, were pinned one by one to the white sheet.

It was a wall of flowers. I remember standing at the back of the club during the wedding reception. In front of the bandstand the wall bloomed, a meadow backing the brass and drums, while the singer sang popular love songs of the day.

The Red Mill traded on the appearance of glamour. There were always flowers on the table for our guests to enjoy. (Red carnations, which were cheaper than roses. But it didn't matter, because we had our own kind of roses: we called the strippers' tassels "tit rosettes.") For the wedding, the impact of those flowers was magnified, perfuming the air. Here was true glamour in the form of nature's astonishing gifts.

* * *

The smell of flowers has never left me. Their scent in the middle of winter is one of my earliest memories. Many years later I was in Moscow, and I noticed that, as poor as they were, the women all wore red carnations. So I bought a red carnation and carried it in the snow on my way to the Bolshoi Ballet. These are the puzzle pieces of memory.

To this day, I burn floral-scented candles at home to remind me of that scent. Dora, my loyal major-domo, arranges flowers in every room of my house. I admire flowers everywhere I go, and I must have them at home. To me, they signal a better life, a more beautiful existence.

Flowers are glamour, yes, but they're also grace. They elevate, and it's elevation that drove me forward in life. The Red Mill created in me a hunger for better things, and it hinted that those things existed somewhere beyond the borders of the Bronx.

CHAPTER 2

"Turn the Lights to Blue, Sonny"

had to grow up fast. I didn't do kid things—for example, I wasn't on a football team. The closest I came to playing a team sport was that running game of stickball with my friends, and that lost its shine pretty quickly.

There was a famous book, *The Amboy Dukes* by Irving Shulman, about tough Jewish street kids in Brooklyn during World War II. In the novel, the gang used a garage as a clubroom. For a brief period in my life, when I was about twelve or thirteen, we had a clubroom. I don't remember the name of the club, but it was a bunch of fellas and it wasn't that much fun. We had some strange sexual experiences there, even stranger than the one my dad had orchestrated to usher me into manhood. But that's a story for a different time.

Percy's Pool Room had far greater appeal. I belonged at the Red Mill, which would have been enough for most boys, but I *wanted* to belong at Percy's Pool Room. Percy's was where everyone would go to smoke joints (we called it "reefer" in those days). There was a lot of marijuana and other drugs at Percy's, and the guys there would play numbers. Everyone would bet. It was simple: gamblers picked numbers and won. The guys running the numbers game would hide the numbers, the actual papers, in the Coke machine at Percy's.

Because I was so innocent looking, I was charged with the task of hiding the numbers in the Coke machine for the guys. In a twist of fate, as an adult I would go on to do a deal with the Coca-Cola Company. It would be the largest deal of my life—a deal that would be worth over a billion dollars today. But back then, when I thought of Coca-Cola, it was only to quench my thirst or keep the cops from finding those numbers. Later, I figured out that the cops knew.

Naturally, I wasn't supposed to hang out at Percy's. Just because my dad worked at a strip club didn't mean he didn't have a sense of propriety—especially when it came to his son. He made his feelings clear about me going over there, but wanting to be one of the guys, I went anyway.

One afternoon, my father left work early, found I wasn't at home, and came looking for me at Percy's, which was walking distance from our apartment. He pushed his way into the main poolroom and crept up to my side, whispering into my ear, "I'm gonna embarrass you so much, you'll never come back." Then he kicked my legs out from under me, and I fell to my knees. He was right: I was embarrassed. He didn't kick me hard, but I got the message.

"You ever gonna come back here again? I don't think so," he said. He grabbed me by the collar and pulled me out onto University Avenue. I was so humiliated. There was this guy at Percy's named Wanz (in Yiddish, "wanz" means "bedbug"), and he didn't want me to come back to the pool hall either. Even the resident bedbug thought I'd be better off at the Red Mill.

At the Red Mill, my father could keep an eye on me. He could control me. Nobody there would have given me drugs—the Red Mill was classier than that. And if I was going to have sexual experiences either way, at least at the Red Mill they'd be clean.

As it turned out, I would learn a series of useful skills there, like photography, lighting, and how to set a table. It was my version of the Boy Scouts or 4-H. And in those instructions were important lessons about glamour.

When I was fifteen or sixteen, one of my jobs was to turn the lights to blue during a key moment in the show. I did this by sliding a blue gel over the lighting can. "Turn the lights to blue, Sonny," the house manager would say, and as the blue gel clicked into place, a low, dusky light would descend upon the stage, dropping a veil of mystery over the room. It was as if I had set an eclipse into motion with only a slight gesture. In that moment, an artificial night fell over the Red Mill.

Then the stripper would start to twirl, and the music would swell. Just as she pulled off the tit rosettes, I'd turn off the lights—the stage had to go black—and the woman would leave the stage.

There was that innocence again. Strippers would end up in pasties and string bikinis, but they'd cover themselves up with great big feathers. There was nary a nipple to be seen, and the patrons couldn't touch them. While there are plenty of places today where women will follow you wherever you want to go for a little cash (all you have to do is tell them to call you at the hotel after their shift), none of that existed back then—and of course we were still decades away from online pornography. The show we put on wasn't salacious—it was more of a tease. And to me, the glamour of it all was more impactful than the whispers of sex anyway.

Glamour, of course, is relative. What was glamorous in the Bronx in the 1940s and '50s—a little mood lighting, a cast of intriguing characters, and some tassels—wasn't true glamour, but I didn't know that. Nonetheless, the Red Mill was shinier than all of the rest of Jerome Avenue put together.

It's important to remember, too, that in those days, burlesque wasn't what it's become today. At a burlesque club, one saw comedians and singers, as well as the dancers. Music and comedy was as big a part of the evening's entertainment as the girls at the end. There'd be a song to open, to bring the house up, and at the end, a song to bring us down. Everyone wanted to be like Minsky's, the famous burlesque hall on the Lower East Side that set the bar for racy strip shows in the early part of the twentieth century. The 1968 movie *The Night They Raided Minsky's*, a zany musical comedy, is set there. The cops were always raiding Minsky's in a futile attempt to keep the neighborhood clean.

The Red Mill was dazzling, but it wouldn't have had to do much to impress me. We were very poor. My father didn't make much money at the Red Mill, so he drove a taxicab on the side. Dad was a giver. He always did favors for people. He never hesitated to give them some of what he had—and occasionally, that got him into trouble.

One night, he stopped to help someone change a tire on West 57th Street. While he was bolting on the tire, he was hit by another car and broke his femur. The break was so bad he was hospitalized, and when he was released, he was weeks away from being able to walk on his own. Our apartment was on the fourth floor and there was no elevator. So Nat Kaye, the Red Mill's owner and a gorilla of a man, put my dad in a chair and carried him upstairs. This was the same Nat Kaye who wouldn't give his permission for my family to hold my bar mitzvah at the Red Mill, and yet here he was, lifting my father, one stair at a time, up four full flights to our home.

I never knew why he did either thing, the hurtful or the generous. It was never discussed. To the Kayes, the Schwartzes were never part of the family, and I never knew them very well. To them, I was just "Sonny." To me, they were sophisticated men in suits and ties who called my dad a demeaning nickname.

But maybe I was wrong. I was never sure which was the more accurate reflection of our relationship with the Kayes: the daily slight of "Schwartzy," or the heroic gesture of Nat carrying my father up the stairs.

Nat Kaye could afford to hire medics to get my father home. Two ambulance drivers would have done the job for not very much money. Maybe he really did care about my dad, too much to let someone else handle the task of transporting him. Or perhaps he was trying to show what a great guy he was, displaying my father's helplessness while highlighting his own heroics. Maybe in that moment, he was robbing my father of his dignity, much the same way he did when he refused to let him hold my bar mitzvah at the Red Mill.

If we ever need to learn how we came to make the choices we've made, there's a map that shows us the way. It's not a map to new worlds, but the route back to that other country where we were made—the past.

My father would walk with a limp for the rest of his life.

* * *

Sometimes I felt desperate to find a place of my own. My family's apartment was achingly small, and the Red Mill was crowded and busy, even when it was closed. Besides, at the Red Mill I was "Schwartzy's kid," not my own person. The personalities at the Red

Mill sucked up all the air in the room, all those big guys staking their turf, and the girls competing for attention. Every once in a while I needed to breathe, and when that mood hit, the Metropolitan Museum of Art in Manhattan offered pure oxygen.

I would take the D train from the Tremont Avenue station to Manhattan and walk from the stop at Lexington Avenue over to the Met. Once inside the museum, with its high ceilings, polished floors, and hushed galleries, I'd enter my own imaginary world. I particularly liked the knights in shining armor; I made up stories about them, and those were my movies. I looked at paintings by Renoir and Degas. I learned about art. It was a nice place to be.

It turned out I wasn't the only member of my family plagued by the urge to escape. When I was seventeen, my mother, Ruth Eisler, ran away—all the way to Florida, about as far as she could get on a train from Penn Station. Worse, she had me bring her to the station. I was the one who had to break the news to my dad.

Years later, someone said, "I guess you were abandoned." I'd never thought of it as abandonment, but that's what it was.

I realize now that my mother was living an unhappy life, and it just wasn't her nature to accept the hand she'd been dealt. She was pretty eccentric to begin with, studying Buddhism and Christian Science, nothing like the typical Jewish housewives in the Bronx. She was exotic, kind of a hippie for her day. She did what she wanted and never made excuses for it. For example, I'd always thought we kept kosher—but we ate bacon. When I realized that counted as a transgression, I asked my mother about it. She simply replied, "It's good for you."

My mother was born in Budapest. When she was about ten years old, her family sent her to America alone to live with relatives in Chicago. My father was born in Manhattan, on the Lower East Side, and grew up in Brooklyn. They met in New York at a dime-a-dance hall. Like the song says, "Ten cents a dance, that's what they pay me."

Ruth was daring and beautiful. Everyone agreed that she looked like Ingrid Bergman. I can still see her sitting in the back of the Red Mill drinking a manhattan, sipping it slowly and looking off into the distance, just like Ilsa, Bergman's character in *Casablanca*. Perhaps she was remembering a song she used to hear as a girl in Budapest.

But while she may have been different than other Jewish mothers, she certainly had the guilt thing down. One time, she took me to Coney Island, a big, expensive trip we didn't make often. On our way home, we stopped at the Horn & Hardart Automat in Washington Heights. I loved the feeling of putting a coin into one of the slots and pulling out my chicken pot pie or peach cobbler. The food was delicious, made with the best ingredients, and because there were no waiters to pay, it cost less than what you'd find at most restaurants. I was so charmed by the experience, particularly the hot drink dispensers, which were shaped like lion's heads. Coffee and hot chocolate poured from their mouths.

That day, my mother didn't eat anything. She just sat there, sipping her hot chocolate as the wind blew against the window, threatening snow. Meanwhile, my tray was piled high—a hamburger, Salisbury steak, mac and cheese, the huckleberry pie I loved—all paid for with nickels, dimes, and quarters. After I ate, we left the restaurant. It was freezing outside, but my mother insisted we walk across the Washington Bridge to Andrews Avenue in the Bronx. This was no casual stroll around the block: it would take at least an hour, probably more, but she liked to walk. She told me the fresh air was good for me. As we trudged on, the icy gusts coming off the Hudson, I asked, "Why didn't you eat? Weren't you hungry?"

"I didn't want to," she said.

"What do you mean you didn't want to?"

"I didn't have enough money."

"We could have shared," I told her.

She shook her head. I began feeling a familiar, complex stew of guilt and anger. Guilt because she hadn't eaten and now we'd be walking a long way in the cold, and anger because, even as I felt guilty, I knew that was her intention. She wanted me to feel that way.

"Well, how much did you need?" I asked her. I dug my hands into my pockets, fingering the coins the strippers, bartenders, and Sam tipped me for helping out around the Red Mill.

"A penny," she replied.

"You needed a penny? That's all?"

Why didn't she say something? I wondered. Surely she'd known that I had a few coins in my pocket. Then again, I hadn't told her I had the money. *Was it a test? Did she want me to offer her what I had while she sat there not eating?* If so, I'd obviously failed. But I was just a kid.

We were mostly silent for the rest of the walk. I kept glancing at her, bracing against the cold, feeling the guilt and frustration flood through me. A penny.

* * *

When she ran away, she ended up in Miami. To go after her, my father had to borrow money from the Chinese cook at the Red Mill.

It wasn't easy, but he eventually found her, and they returned to the Bronx together. It probably would have been better for everyone if she'd stayed in Miami and he'd come home alone.

A little while after they returned, my mother found a matchbook in my father's pocket; the phone number of one of the strippers was written on it. My mother tied the matchbook up with string and a bow, like a present, and dangled it in front of him for the rest of their lives.

Like I said, maybe it would have been OK if she'd stayed in Miami.

* * *

Because of our circumstances I always felt inadequate and insecure. I suppose I was embarrassed. I never told George Wood about my father's work, and I'd worry that my father would be the one to pull up whenever we hailed a cab. I felt uncomfortable in George's glamorous world, even as I yearned to join it.

I was born on Davidson Avenue (before my family moved), next to the steps that led down to Macombs Road and onto Jerome Avenue. Those steps have been made famous in the film *Joker*, where the title character is shown dancing on them, and they've now become a tourist attraction. What dangerous fun we'd have in the snow, sledding down the sides of those steps.

The apartment in which I grew up seemed bare and unfurnished. We didn't have many things, and we certainly didn't have nice things. Later, when I'd visit the luxurious apartments of Mr. Lastfogel (William Morris's president), Sammy Davis Jr., or even George Wood himself, I would come to understand just how threadbare my childhood home had been.

I've never liked the feeling of victimhood, though. I dwell on what I've done—for better or for worse—but never on what I don't have. The story of my life isn't one of deprivation. My situation was no different from those of countless others. It was just circumstances, and the circumstances were that my family didn't have a lot.

There are people who use their circumstances to succeed. They take their past experiences and use them as fuel, propelling themselves

29

somewhere else—somewhere better. Then they say, "I was a victim, and look what I did to overcome all that." That's one way to go about life. Other people accept their lot and move on.

That's what I did: I accepted my lot. At least, that's what I told myself. Now I see that I worked hard to overcome my circumstances and create new ones. It was up to me to create change, despite my lot. We're formed by our history, but we have the ability to make decisions that will form our future.

My father tried to be as responsible as he could. He didn't steal, and he didn't sell or use drugs. When my mother left, he thought it was his duty to bring her back. Within a corrupt world, he stayed true to his belief that no matter how strong the surrounding forces of dissolution may be, the strength of individuals is more powerful. He had a code, and it made sense to me.

Watching George Wood, I learned a lot about the importance of codes, but not at first. At first, I just liked those alligator shoes a lot.

CHAPTER 3

The Mailroom

Before I met George Wood, the figure who held the most glamour for me was Moe Gold. Nobody is named Moe anymore, or Irving or Max . . . or Murray, for that matter. Moe Gold was small-time theatrical agent who carried what was called a "Jewish bankroll." Guys would carry a wad of cash with a $100 bill on top (Moe Gold probably used a $20); underneath the large bill would be lots of singles, to plump it up. That's a Jewish bankroll.

To me, Moe Gold was a hero. He had all these broads hanging around. He had pin-striped suits. He had a big wad of dough. What *more* would I want in life? What more do some guys want in life? Guys want a snappy suit, and these days, maybe some tats. They want a big bankroll. They want women to go crazy for them because they're bad boys. It's the same today as it was back then—it hasn't ever changed.

In retrospect, Moe was kind of a sleazy guy. There were always cigar ashes on his suit jacket. But what did I know? It was Moe who told me about the William Morris Agency. "The Red Mill isn't for you, kid," he said.

At the time, I was finishing high school. I never graduated, going instead for my GED. I'd never been encouraged in any direction, not academically or in any other way. No one had ever suggested I try anything in particular—not even playing an instrument. Nothing. I was a blank canvas, just like those nightclub tablecloths before we fastened the flowers to them. So I began to search for direction on my own.

I'd already made it out a little ways. One summer I got a job as a waiter at Camp Onota, a summer camp in Pittsfield, Massachusetts, near the site of the Tanglewood Music Festival. It was my first true vacation. My duties were to help serve the family in the main dining room. The rest of the time I could enjoy what the campers did all summer. It was like having my own summer home. I saw the ballet and heard the philharmonic conducted by Leonard Bernstein. I experienced modern dance for the first time and heard people talk about books and philosophy. Over the summer, I became close to the wealthy family who owned the camp, and after the season was over, they invited me to stay on and help out.

One night a friend and I captured a jar of fireflies and took them to a nearby movie theater. The feature was *High Noon*, starring Gary Cooper and Grace Kelly, whom I'd get to know many years later in Monte Carlo, when she was Princess Grace of Monaco. Once the house lights went down, we released the fireflies into the darkened theater, where they twinkled like stars above the heads of the audience. It was magical. And it was the beginning of my creativity, of capturing magic and letting it loose.

That was the summer before I went to the William Morris Agency, and it helped to prime me for something—*anything*—other than the life I'd had so far. So when Moe mentioned William Morris, I was more than ready to entertain the idea.

All these years later, I can see how desperate I was to experience more than what I'd learned at the Red Mill and in the Bronx. I wanted more beauty in my life. It felt like a true necessity, and the desire to achieve it drew me to Manhattan, and to entertainment.

We all want things in our lives that last: ideas, relationships, creations, even products. And that's why—then and now—I search for the transcendent, beautiful or otherwise. What transcends, lasts. It isn't snobbery, although I do love aesthetics. What I learned growing up in the Bronx is that life needed to contain more, to *be* more. Reaching for more makes *us* more. It was a revelation to discover that there was something bigger than the Red Mill.

And so I got on a subway train one afternoon and presented myself at the William Morris Agency. There I met Sid Feinberg, who was what these days we'd call the head of HR. He was a conventional guy, nothing like the flashy types who did the deals. It was an easy interview. Back when I was still in school, I'd had a job for a little while delivering the mail at ABC, and that was good enough for Sid. Soon I had a job in the mailroom.

Many years later, right before William Morris merged with Endeavor, Norman Brokaw and I were having lunch. He invited me up to the office and asked me to tell him what had changed since my days in the mailroom. My answer: "a lot." Back in the fifties, I'd carried a heavy bag that strained my shoulder and pulled at my clothes, and here these guys were, rolling their fancy carts around. All of them were from rich Beverly Hills families, well dressed, with Rolex watches adorning their wrists. Some of my mailroom pals had been wealthy, sure . . . but they were still *hungry*. None of these guys seemed to have the same drive. Moreover, I doubted the bowels of that building held the same cast of characters I'd encountered in my days carting mail to some of the country's top agents.

On the *The Merv Griffin Show* we used to do theme shows. We had a running joke that Merv had run out of themes, and so his theme the next night would be people who like broccoli. I once went to Merv and said, "Why don't we gather all of these guys and do an episode about the boys in the mailroom?"

"It's too New York," he said. "No one will get it." I'm not quite sure he was right.

This wasn't like any other mailroom job. It was the most prestigious mailroom job in the world. Throughout history, many future industry leaders have been trained in the William Morris mailroom—big names like Ron Meyer, Irwin Winkler, David Geffen, Mike Ovitz, and Barry Diller. And Murray Schwartz.

One of my mailroom buddies was David Niven Jr., the son of the smooth British actor David Niven. One day we went to lunch together at the Stage Deli. He was complaining about life as David Niven Jr., living at the Hotel St. Moritz on Central Park South and dating famous actresses.

After I'd listened to him bitch about his existence for long enough, I laughed and said, "You should try life as Murray Schwartz from the Bronx. You might be happier."

David and I used to go to the Horn & Hardart Automat at 56th Street and Sixth Avenue. Unlike the main Automat in Times Square, this one was only a counter. David loved the mac and cheese, which to him was terribly exotic, a real delicacy. He'd order it in his upper-class English accent, which was pretty damn funny to me. We may have lived very different lives, but the guys in the mailroom certainly made for interesting conversation partners.

Irwin Winkler, another mailroom guy, became an incredible director and producer, making over fifty movies, including *Rocky*, *Raging Bull*, *The Right Stuff*, and *Goodfellas*. He was a very nice guy, and we palled around. He and I, together with his wife, Margo, and my then-wife, Ann, once went on a picnic to Jones Beach, just to get out of city. There we were, these stark white bodies that had never seen any sunshine.

There was also Bernie Brillstein, a smart, gregarious, heavyset guy with the biggest laugh of anyone I've ever known. Bernie would go on to become a talent agent and film and television producer. His credits include *The Blues Brothers*, *Ghostbusters*, and *Happy Gilmore*, as well as the beloved television shows *Hee Haw*, *The Muppet Show*, and *The Sopranos*. He would also cofound Brillstein-Grey Entertainment, a tremendously successful talent management and production company in Hollywood.

Jerry Tokofsky was another guy I got to be friendly with. We were never really buddies—after all, what if he got the job I wanted? Instead of forging a real bond, we mostly gossiped. Jerry was a good-looking guy, more of a movie star than an agent, but he eventually became a producer, making movies like *Glengarry Glen Ross*.

Harry Kalcheim, one of the Kalcheim brothers, was known as a great talent guy at William Morris, and he had all of us young kids running around town bringing people in. Then he would take the credit. Nevertheless, it was my job and I loved it. It was a monumental improvement over delivering the mail.

I befriended Marty Litke shortly after joining the mailroom staff. He was just a nice guy from Brooklyn, quieter than the other guys—and I was a quiet kid myself, so we got along well. Marty and I discovered some serious talent together, including Bill Cosby and Barbra Streisand.

I remember the night we first saw Streisand. We went down to the Bon Soir, a tiny nightclub in Greenwich Village. It had a small stage and low ceilings, making the little light there was down there harsh. On that stage was a girl singer with a face I couldn't quite describe as pretty, but she still exuded femininity. She was sexy in a way I hadn't seen before. Her hands and fingers almost had a voice of their own, and with her eyes she connected with everyone in the audience. She already knew how to play a crowd. She had the presence of the big stars we represented.

I don't remember exactly what kind of band she had; it wasn't more than a trio—piano, bass, and drums maybe. She looked like a hippie, and while she wasn't what I'd call attractive—certainly not compared to the girls at the Red Mill—wow, could she sing.

Marty and I saw talent all the time, and when she took the stage and started singing, we knew we'd found it. She just sparkled. We gave our cards to her manager, and the next day, we told Harry what we'd seen. When he saw her, he knew she was the real deal. And as usual, he took credit for finding her.

We discovered Cosby in a similar manner. His manager, an ex-ad guy named Roy Silver, told us we had to check him out. "He's going to be a star, I'm telling you," he insisted. Cosby was performing at the Gaslight Café, another dark place you had to go down a flight of stairs to get into. Roy had signed Bob Dylan after seeing him at the Gaslight, though he'd since sold Dylan's contract to Albert Grossman.[1] Marty and I figured it was worth a shot.

When we arrived, there was Cosby, sitting on a stool. I was

---

[1] Frank Rose, *The Agency: William Morris and the Hidden History of Show Business* (New York: Harper Business, 1996).

expecting something dirty to come out of his mouth when he grabbed the microphone, but the jokes were clean. He was intelligent, and as funny as could be. I knew that he was made for TV. We brought him in, and Harry signed him right away.

Harry never let on that the discovery had been ours, but that year, out of nowhere, I got a huge bonus: around $25,000. Back then you could buy a house with that. It was a tremendous amount of money to get as a bonus. I couldn't believe it. It must have been Harry's way of acknowledging my contributions.

Marty and I ended up becoming partners. Marty would book talent for the game shows, and I would do it for other ones. When we settled into a shared office together, he ordered a great big glass top for his desk. Under that glass top, he slid pictures of himself, along with letters from friends and colleagues—people who'd written to tell him what a wonderful person he was, how he was a lovely man and good agent.

One day Marty was out to lunch, and I couldn't resist playing a little prank. We'd represented Marcel Marceau, the great mime, and I had a piece of stationery from him. It had his name at the top, along with a picture of him in his mime outfit. I lifted that glass, took out one of Marty's letters, and replaced it with Marcel's stationery—nothing on it, not a word. I laughed about that one for years. George thought it was pretty funny too, calling me to his office to relay it to those who'd stop by.

But my friendship with Marty and the others was the exception to the rule. In general, the mailroom wasn't a place to make friends. All the guys were extremely competitive. Besides, you were rarely in the same place at the same time, unless it was lunchtime, and those lunchtimes varied. You could be out on what was called a trip, delivering contracts—or, if you were low on the totem pole, kinescopes, which were big, heavy cans of video. If there was a sales meeting, you'd have to go to Madison Avenue and deliver the kinescope, your back aching the whole way from the strain.

The lack of free time aside, the guys in the mailroom could be cutthroat, and they did whatever it took to get an edge. One guy would steam open envelopes and read all the executives' mail. Then, in the TV meetings, he'd offer up his insights—heavily influenced by what he'd read—and appear to be an absolute genius. He really *was* a genius, but in those meetings, the help he got from those letters certainly didn't hurt.

Author Frank Rose wrote a book called *The Agency: William Morris and the Hidden History of Show Business*, in which he interviewed some of the biggest names that came out of the William Morris mailroom. Among his subjects was Jeff Wald, who became a manager in his own right. In fact, he worked for me for a little while—though he apparently wasn't too fond of our interactions. In his interview, he describes me as "a pompous prick and a petty despot who hated me and got rid of me in a week. I had opinions and he didn't want to hear them. Murray fired Geffen too." (That last part's not true, by the way. That's a plain old lie.)

He went on to say, "Murray handled the *The Merv Griffin Show*, which in those days wasn't the high end. Then he became president of Merv's company and wound up with millions of dollars when Merv sold out. He's still a prick."[2] You can just hear the tension in that quote, the desire to compete and come out on top even decades after the fact.

---

2 Ibid.

Someone told me I should sue him, but I had other plans. Instead of bringing him to court, I wrote him a letter.

Dear Jeff,

I didn't know you thought I was a petty despot, but one of the reasons I canned you is that you couldn't take letters. I had to take letters, and I didn't want to do it anymore. That's why you shouldn't have come to work for a guy you were going to compete with. Nevertheless, Jeff, the next time I'm in Hawaii with you and your wife, knowing that you thought I was such a prick, I won't be picking up your check.

That was the end of that, but it demonstrates just how aggressive we were with each other.

David Geffen is one of the most famous graduates of the William Morris mailroom, of course. His enthusiasm and need to succeed were unparalleled. Everyone was impressed by his understanding of music and of the business at large. Was he friendly? No. But he had an incredible grasp of how to make deals—I don't know where it came from. From what I recall, he came from Brooklyn and his mother ran a ladies lingerie shop. But he was going to succeed, no matter what.

His approach demonstrates that same sense of competition as Wald's, though he took a slightly different tack: "I just observed those who had accomplished something. Lou White, Wally Jordan, Lee Solomon, Steve Jacobs, Marty Litke, Murray Schwartz, and so I tried to talk to as many of them as I could."[3] He asked himself, *Who is doing well here? Who am I going to look at?*

---

3 Ibid.

A long while later, I was staying at my apartment at the Carlyle in New York City with my golden retriever, Charlie. He was a wonderful dog, and I often flew him back and forth to Los Angeles with me. (I could take him because I flew a line called Regent Air, which was run by the owner of Caesars Palace—in essence, a private aircraft, with individual booths like trains used to have in the old days. Today I wouldn't fly with him; I wouldn't put a dog in the hold.)

That particular day, I was walking Charlie over to Central Park. The night before had been rough, and I hadn't shaved that morning, or taken the time to put on a nice suit. I had just thrown on old, ratty clothes and headed for the door, hoping to get the walk over with as fast as I could.

Of course, my dog decided to take a huge dump on the corner of Fifth Avenue on the way to the park. There was a police car right there, and the cop inside rolled down his window. "Pick it up," he commanded.

Oh my God, I thought, *I forgot to bring the little baggies.* I could feel the cop's eyes boring into me as I patted down my pockets for the nonexistent baggies, so I started rummaging through the closest garbage can to find something—anything—to pick up the big pile of crap next to me. It was humiliating, and just when I thought it couldn't get any worse, I saw David Geffen walking down Fifth Avenue with another guy. David was perfectly dressed and clean-shaven, appropriately prepared to be out in public. Worse, he and his companion were coming directly toward me. David caught my eye as he neared. "Hi, David," I said, unsure of what else to do. But he quickly averted his gaze and walked right past me.

I realized I must have looked pretty bad in the moment, and I wanted to explain myself, so I wrote him a note:

Dear David,

I know you saw me the other day on Fifth Avenue, and I must say, things aren't that bad. I was actually just walking to the park from my apartment at the Carlyle.

David replied, saying that in the moment, he didn't think it was me. "It didn't look like you," he said. It was a cute comment, and it made me feel better about the whole interaction.

But I don't want to lead you to believe that everyone who made it to the mailroom of William Morris became rich and famous. It's not true. A lot of people stayed for just a couple of days. There were plenty of people who felt delivering the mail was beneath them. A lot of them got fired—you could be bounced any minute, particularly if you pissed off an agent. Some went on to take executive roles someplace else or to do managerial jobs and never really made a name for themselves, or any real dough. Far more didn't make it than did.

And some found success, only to fall on hard times later—like Mickey Hanft.

Mickey was the funniest man I've ever seen in my life. He should've been a stand-up comedian rather than a talent manager. When he was very young, he married a sweet Brooklyn gal named Frieda. They were a terrific couple. When he left William Morris, he signed Robbie Robertson and The Band. Years later, he lost The Band as a client, and I decided to hire him.

I was expanding Merv Griffin Enterprises at the time, and I suggested to Merv that we create a management company. Merv thought it was a great idea, so I went ahead and hired Mickey. But I hadn't seen him in years. When he arrived, he looked like a hippie, with a beard and a reefer habit to match. He was stoned all day, smoking grass in the office. Merv couldn't stand it. "Maybe it will help him connect with rock 'n' rollers, bring some great names in for the show," I ventured. But Merv didn't agree.

Eventually, I had to let Mickey go. I was sad to do it, but he wasn't really able to handle the job. He just wasn't functioning—I guess that's why he lost The Band. Later, Mickey changed his name to Mickey McFree and became a cowboy in Arizona. His wife, Frieda, the nice girl from Brooklyn, became Faridi McFree, who was hired to nanny Bob Dylan's children and then became Bob's lover after he and his wife, Sara, divorced. That affair got old, eventually, I guess. One day, I bumped into Faridi in New York City. She'd left the Dylan estate and was living in New York doing secretarial work.

Wally Amos of Famous Amos cookies was another mailroom graduate who went on to enjoy great success—although he ended up struggling later. In his interview for Rose's *The Agency*, Wally said, "I wasn't concerned with the history of William Morris; I was busy trying to get the hell out of the mailroom. I worked all day and went to school at night. I didn't take lunch; I set up a typewriter in a corner of the mailroom and practiced. I figured that when you show initiative, people automatically respond. After two months, I became a floater because my skills were comparable to any of the secretaries'. I worked on many desks and got to prove what Wally Amos was about."[4]

Wally became the first African-American talent agent at William Morris. He was in the nightclub department for a while, and just like they wanted George to work with the Mafia guys in Vegas to exploit his connections—which we'll get into later—they wanted Wally to go up to Harlem. It sounds terrible now, but that was how the world

---

4 Ibid.

was. It was a reality of that time. We've come a long way since those days. He would go on to lead the rock 'n' roll department, and he signed big-deal clients like Simon and Garfunkel, Diana Ross, the Supremes, Sam Cooke, and Marvin Gaye.

Back in the mailroom, before he was promoted, Wally would bring cookies for everyone—his grandma's recipe. We had a coffeepot down there too, and people would hang around, drinking endless cups of coffee and munching on those cookies.

One day, Wally told us he was going to leave his coveted role as a talent agent to pursue his cookie business. "Wally, why don't you stay at the William Morris Agency?" I asked. But it worked out for him—at least at first.

Wally started his company with a $25,000 loan from Marvin Gaye and Helen Reddy, who just happened to be Jeff Wald's wife.[5] He was the first guy to develop a premium cookie, and boy, were they delicious. I used to love when they gave out those little yellow bags on airplanes. Thinking about them, I can almost taste that first crunchy bite—the satisfyingly sandy texture and just a hint of salt to balance all that sweetness.

But Wally was never a great businessman; he didn't learn from his time at William Morris. He was living the good life in Hawaii, and every time he needed cash, he'd sell off a little piece of Famous Amos, until he didn't own anything anymore—not even his own image. Just a few years ago he tried to pitch a new cookie idea on *Shark Tank*, because he didn't have the resources to launch it on his own. The sharks didn't bite.

---

5 Dana Canedy, "A Famous Cookie and a Face to Match: How Wally Amos Got His Hand and His Name Back in the Game," *New York Times*, July 3, 1999.

The mailroom was a conglomeration of unique individuals—fellas who wanted to do something with their lives. Some succeeded and some didn't, but all of us were affected by that place in some way. So much so that not long ago, I found myself wondering how I fit in and stood out, and how I'd made a name for myself at William Morris and beyond.

After a lot of soul-searching, I realized that, despite the fact I was brought up in the Red Mill alongside strippers and other rough stuff, I was also more cloistered than the other guys. They seemed much more worldly than I was. For example, take Jerry Weintraub, another kid from the Bronx. He managed concert tours for Elvis Presley, Frank Sinatra, the Four Seasons, and many others, and produced films like *Diner* and *The Karate Kid*. He was kind of a fast talker, and I felt like I'd never be like him. We were around the same age, but I think he thought of me as a kid.

After thinking about it for a long time, I realized why. Sure, I'd been exposed to things that many of those other guys hadn't been, but I wasn't out in the world as much as they were . . . until I met George Wood, that is.

CHAPTER 4

George, the Boys, and Me

As far as I was concerned, that first impression George made on me was the beginning of his story as well as mine. I've always thought about people not in terms of height, weight, or color—but presence. My dad didn't look short to me, and I certainly didn't think of myself that way. Perhaps it was because I didn't see myself as short that I had the chutzpah to walk into William Morris in the first place.

In fact, I never even thought about my height until I dated a woman named Sylvia. Sylvia was beautiful and elegant, and she was tall. I met her at Neiman Marcus, where she sold gifts. One day we went to a party together, a big Hollywood bash in Beverly Hills. She said, "You know, you're a petite guy."

"Petite?" I said. "There's nothing petite about me. I may not be tall, but I'm not short."

George Wood had presence. His style made him seem very tall, although he wasn't.

It took me some time to understand that at the agency, appearances—George's included—were not to be trusted. Behind the shiny shoes, slicked-back hair, and even slicker talk were worries, debts, and the exhaustion that comes from trying to maintain a front full time.

In my day, so many guys lived on hope. They never really made a lot of dough. Only the entrepreneurs raked in the big bucks. Agency salaries were nice, but they weren't astronomical. Instead of money, we had expense accounts, free travel, open tabs at the top restaurants in town, and rooms at the best hotels in the world.

Guys were willing to give up a lot of their spirit and personal integrity in exchange for those perks. The perks were what set us apart from other people . . . and I very much wanted to be set apart from other people.

At the agency, expense accounts were handled by a woman named Jeanne Petrono. On Fridays, we would go see Jeanne and hand in our expenses. If Jeanne liked you, she wouldn't question what you turned in and would simply hand you the cash, rolled up in a yellow envelope. I could do as I pleased, and that was good enough for me.

But that wasn't the case for a lot of other guys, and it certainly wasn't the case for George. As I came to see, George struggled more than anyone else there. He was often in a financial panic brought on by his gambling losses. All those fancy dinners did nothing to pay back his debts. Instead, his life was driven by one question: *Where am I going to get more money so that I can gamble again?*

I wanted to tell him to quit gambling. I wanted to say, "You have so much to live for. With your contacts, you could be a great agent, but you have no accounts. Why are you squandering your life?"

With no accounts to speak of, you may be wondering why William Morris kept George around. It was an open secret that George's value lay in his links to the Mafia. He was the agency's emissary to the mob. Staying available for them was paramount. It wouldn't have worked too well had Frank Costello or Meyer Lansky called George only to find him in a meeting discussing schedules or contracts. Even if he'd had a head for the procedural stuff, it wasn't what might be called his "best and highest use."

He also had another role, one as the agency's fixer, as it were. Wood was the go-to when celebrities went crazy and the deals got complicated. For instance, after Frank Sinatra was found in the elevator of his building with his wrists slashed, the agency higher-ups called George. When Sinatra and his wife Ava Gardner were in the throes of a dramatic, scandalous Hollywood divorce, it was George Wood who kept him from going off the deep end. George stayed by his side day and night during the weeks when Sinatra was hungover from the knockdown, drag-out fights with Gardner and out of his mind with jealousy. George was his shadow. Wherever he went, George wasn't far behind.

During his early years at William Morris, George took care of the big acts like Jimmy Durante and Danny Thomas, Sophie Tucker and Joe E. Lewis. He was a "handler" right out of the gate, and he was good at it. Dealing with mercurial celebrity talent was an art, and Wood was one of the great masters. He could be therapist, cajoler, or tough guy, depending on what the situation called for, and that skill set helped him keep celebrities out of the headlines and on the stage.

I certainly didn't understand that at the time, so I was baffled by George's choices—and his place there.

But George was a mystery to me in general. I knew very little about his life before he joined William Morris—just that he'd been a small-time talent manager, arriving at the agency from someplace he didn't want to talk about.

Sometimes, his day started at five in the evening, but most of the time, he sauntered in at eleven or noon. He never went to meetings, and he didn't really answer to anyone except for Abe Lastfogel and his friends in the Mafia. He had a standing appointment at the Essex House Barbershop for a shave and a trim every evening.

George and I lived in worlds that were alien to each other, but I recognized later that he and I came from similarly hard backgrounds. He'd grown up on the Lower East Side, like my father. Eventually, I'd learn that George was embarrassed by his own father, Joe, who was rough around the edges in a way that was familiar to me.

George never knew about my upbringing, but I realize now that, under the surface, our similarities created an unspoken language. I believe now that my scrappiness would have appealed to that side of him, and that focusing on what we had in common would have brought us closer. But that didn't really happen—at least not right away.

Once I started to work for George, I knew I would need to learn a lot, and fast. His personality was enormous, big enough to fill rooms and make an indelible mark on the lives of those around him. The irony is that an average day with George Wood could be quite mundane—boring, even. In between placing bets, conferring with mobsters, making promises to starlets, and being measured for suits, he didn't do much.

Each morning, George would arrive at the office carrying the *Herald Tribune*, the important paper of the day. He'd lean back in his chair, cross his feet on top of his desk, and snap open the paper, reading it cover to cover. He didn't want to answer to anyone and he didn't like the office routine, so he just ignored it.

George's indolence ended up working for me, though. I was "the kid," George's secretary, but I learned to do a lot in a short amount of time because George did so little. Contracts would arrive on his desk, only to be dropped onto mine. "Take a look at this," he'd say. "Let me know if it's any good." Over time, I became adept at understanding the details within the contracts and could read them as well as any agent. This fluency with contracts enabled me to make my biggest career strides. Making deals is what agents do, and I loved it.

And then there were the parts of my job that were specific to George—the things the other assistants didn't do for their bosses. One night as he was leaving the office, George stopped by my desk: "Don't leave until Jimmy B. phones." I soon learned that Jimmy B. was Vincent "Jimmy Blue Eyes" Alo, the famous mob figure. One was not to call him "Jimmy Blue Eyes," however. George could call him Jimmy, but I was to refer to him as "Mr. Alo."

"I won't go anywhere," I said. "You can count on me." And I did just that. I waited for Jimmy's call.

It's hard to believe there once was a time when people waited *by* the phone. And I waited all right. I waited and waited, afraid to move for fear of missing that important call. One by one, everyone left for the day. There I sat, alone in the silence of an empty office at 7 p.m., my desk lamp casting shadows on the walls.

By ten o' clock, Jimmy B. still hadn't called. I was starving, so I called the Stage Deli and had a pastrami sandwich delivered. At midnight, still nothing. Then it was 3:00 a.m., and still no phone call. At some point, I fell asleep on the sofa in George's office.

Around 10 a.m., George came in. By then I was sitting at my desk, but I was dressed in the same clothes I'd been wearing the day before. George looked confused. "What are you still doing here?" he asked.

"You told me not to leave until he phoned," I said.

"You waited?"

"I waited all night. Jimmy didn't call." George picked up the phone, dialed, and when the party on the other end answered, he said, "Jimmy, the kid is still here because you forgot to call. I told you he'd wait." I'd become somebody he could trust, and he wasn't a very trusting guy.

I now believe that George got a tip that his office was going to be bugged that night, so he planted me there to keep anyone from coming in to place the device. He had reason to be careful, as his office ultimately *would* be bugged—twice, in fact. In 1959, Manhattan District Attorney Frank Hogan was investigating the fixing of boxing matches by Anthony "Fat Tony" Salerno. Salerno had threatened boxing promoter Bill Rosensohn to get him to sell Salerno his company. Because Salerno lived in Florida, Hogan couldn't legally bug his phone, so Hogan bugged George's phone instead. Hogan's guys put the bug under the arm of George's office chair.

They heard a lot, especially when it came to George's treatment of young actresses. George used to say to the girls, "In this business, baby, it's not how good you are, it's who you know. The guys who control the industry are all friends of mine." Let's just say George fixed up a lot of dates.

But that doesn't mean they got the whole story. Because George knew how close to trouble he operated, he had a lot of rules about what I could and couldn't say on the phone, and he was careful about what was discussed in the office. In retrospect, I think that's why I wasn't allowed to say "Jimmy Blue Eyes." I realize that George was worried about being followed. By the time George was bugged again, this time by the order of Attorney General Robert Kennedy, I was long gone.

That wasn't the only time my loyalty would be put to the test. George used to like to go to the fights on Friday night with his buddy, a man named Sugar Brown. Sugar was a short little bald guy, but he had the best name I'd ever heard, which was saying something after growing up with the characters at the Red Mill. Sugar T. Todd Brown was his full name, and his nickname, of course, was Shug.

One time, George had to go to Italy to deliver a package. He didn't want anybody to know what the trip was about, but I knew. He was paying a visit to Joe Adonis, the major Italian American mob figure who'd had a hand in forming the modern Cosa Nostra, Sicily's own crime syndicate.

The trip must have been important, because George would miss a big fight while he was away. He gave me his front-row ticket. It was to be a boys' night out: Champ Segal; Sugar; Henry Gine, a "theatrical manager" with a permanently stiff neck; and me. Henry told me why his neck was so stiff: he'd been shot there, and as a result, he walked with his head cocked to one side at all times. All of the boys were dapper, except for Champ Segal, who was sloppy and always soiled. He was nothing like the rest of them, who prided themselves on looking sharp.

George had given me $500 before getting on the plane for Italy and instructed me to bet whatever way Sugar wanted me to bet. I'd never been to a fight before, and we sat up front. It was terribly exciting. Sugar had told me to bring a newspaper, and I did, though I had no idea why. When I got there, I learned that the purpose of the newspaper was to block any blood that would spatter us in the front row.

After we took our seats, Sugar leaned over to me and said, "Put the dough in your pocket, and tell George he lost. We'll split it. Don't worry about it."

"No," I said.

"I'm *telling* you to do it," Shug said. "Don't worry."

According to George, Sugar's job was to make the bet, and mine was to follow his lead and enjoy the fight. But I was too nervous to sit back, relax, and take it all in. So I left early and called my father to ask what I should do.

"You gotta tell George when he comes back," he said. "You *must* tell him."

Jimmy B., Sugar Brown, Henry, Champ Segal: these were the people George would have dinner with—his crew—and here I was, about to tell George that one of his best friends had tried to double cross him. Terrific. "Sugar Brown's his best friend," I said. "George is either going to beat the crap out of me or fire me."

In the end, I didn't place the bet. I didn't pocket the money, either. I sometimes wonder what would've happened if I had. He'd have fired me, probably. I guess they would've found another kid in a blue suit.

When George returned from Europe, he said to me, "Did you bet that dough? Did I win?" I was scared to death. This was the most frightening moment of my life up to that point, and I prayed I wouldn't collapse.

I took a deep breath. "I have to tell you a story, Mr. Wood. It's about your bet." George gave me a long, hard stare. I was sure he was going to kill me.

"Did I win, or didn't I?"

"You didn't win or lose," I said slowly. "I didn't place the bet." George stood up. "Sugar isn't as good a friend of yours as you think," I said.

"What do you mean?" said George.

He's going to hit me, I thought, wincing preemptively. This was it. The End. Everything was about to be over before I'd even gotten started.

"I was going to bet," I said. "I swear to you, I was." And then I told him what Sugar had said to me. I told George that his best friend had tried to get me to cheat him. George was quiet.

"Get Sugar on the phone," he said. I called Sugar Brown while I tried not to piss my pants. That's no exaggeration. I was still a kid, and this was the only good job I'd ever had. If I lost this one, where was I going to go? As Sugar picked up the phone, I felt dizzy. I was sure I was going to puke.

"Sugar," I said. With Sugar, it wasn't like it was with Jimmy B. I was allowed to call him by his first name. "It's Mr. Wood." I handed George the receiver. George paused for a moment. He appeared to be choosing his words. Just when I thought I couldn't take it anymore, he spoke.

"He told me," he said. There was another pause. After that came an explosion. George laughed so hard I thought the walls would buckle and the windows would shatter. *What the fuck was going on?*

"I *told* you he'd tell me!" George roared.

George and Shug had set me up. It was a trap, a con . . . and for George, another bet. But I'd passed.

There were other tests. On one occasion, he asked, "What are you doing tonight?" He was big on asking me what I was doing at night. It was usually the lead-in to request a favor, and George learned quickly that I rarely had evening plans. That day was no different. "I've got nothing going on," I told him.

"Good. You have to go upstate to deliver a package to Red from Utica." Red from Utica was a local bookmaker I'd met several times in New York with George. George owed him a lot of money, and Red wanted it fast.

George called me into his office and gestured toward a suitcase. "Open that and take a look," he said. It was filled with cash—a lot, by the look of it, though George never told me how much was in there. Before I left, George took me out for a drink. "Take care of yourself, kid," he said. "By the way, you look great tonight." I was wearing a beige balmacaan raincoat. A trench coat would've been too on the nose.

He hugged me and said goodbye. It was the closest we'd ever been, George and I.

I was his surrogate, a young, honest kid embarking on a dangerous mission. And it *was* dangerous, in more ways than one. After the send-off from George, I flew to Utica, New York, in bad weather in a double-prop plane, and delivered the cash to Red.

I thought it was the most exciting thing I'd ever done in my life. I felt like I was in a Humphrey Bogart movie; the scene was terribly noir. I held the briefcase on my lap throughout the flight, and when I got off, Red was waiting on the tarmac in a car with his buddies.

Red from Utica looked just like the actor James Gandolfini in his role as Tony Soprano. Actors who play mobsters seem to be cast in line with the real guys, not just to fulfill stock type. Red had always liked me, and the boys in Utica were the nicest guys I'd ever met. I stayed overnight at Red's house, and they took me out for a sensational Italian dinner. It was a wonderful trip. Perhaps I loved it because it felt like an extension of the Red Mill. It was part of the milieu I knew and understood.

It was on that trip that I began to learn that George really didn't have any money. I also began to realize that, even though I'd proven myself trustworthy time after time, I wouldn't ever get as close to George Wood as I'd hoped. He was never as warm to me again as he'd been that night. But he continued to count on me for help when it came to "business."

George started to send me to see the boys pretty often. He asked me to go see Jules Podell, a tough guy who ran the Copacabana, one of the most important and glamorous nightclubs in New York. The Copa is still legendary.

At the Morris office we had something called an "availability list," which was printed daily. This was before the use of computers, so each day, a secretary typed out an alphabetized list of the talent available to be booked at nightclubs.

One day, George handed me the list. "Go over to the Poodle's place." Figuring out George's codes was part of the job, and I quickly discerned that Poodle was Podell. "Take the list and tell me who he wants and when he wants them."

So I went over to the Copa and met Jules Podell. On his pinkie he wore a large ruby ring surrounded by diamonds. George didn't do bling. His jewelry was limited to a slender Audemars Piguet watch and small gold cuff links. But the Poodle wasn't going to run his show with understated pieces. He needed to let people know who was the boss, and flash was the clearest messenger.

At night, the Copa was the most thrilling, glamorous place, filled with beautiful women in satin gowns and elegant men in dark suits with their hair slicked back. The tables sparkled with champagne bubbling in chilled flutes. The waxed and buffed dance floor shone brightly.

On the bandstand were the most famous names in show business, beaming under the spotlight. But by day, with the house lights up, the place looked seedy. You could see the stains on the banquettes and the scuffs on the floor. This was something else I'd learned at the Red Mill. During the day, all clubs look sleazy, run-down, and dull. It's the nighttime itself that gives them glamour.

I remember sitting with the Poodle and feeling nervous. Like all the guys George sent me to see, the Poodle was scary. These people played by a different set of rules.

Even so, I couldn't help but be enamored of them. I loved the way the boys dressed. They wore beautiful custom clothing, and almost all of them were well manicured. When they spoke, though, it was quite the contrast. Those perfectly tailored suits couldn't cover up the raw, uneducated mannerisms of their speech. "You want something to drink?" Jules asked. "You old enough to drink?" It was a put-down. He knew I was old enough to drink, but he had to assert his authority, to make me squirm and feel weak.

"I am old enough, but I'm not having any," I said.

"Did George tell you not to drink?" Jules responded.

"No," I said. "*I* know not to." I was getting smart. I knew to keep my head clear. I pulled out the list, and Jules leaned in.

"Sammy Davis, where is he the week of May twentieth?"

"I'm sorry Mr. Podell, he's not available that week," I said. I was respectful and professional when I said it, but it was the wrong answer. Podell slammed his fist on the table. "When you go back, tell George Sammy's available."

I don't know how it happened, but somehow, magically, Sammy was at the Copa on May twentieth. I often wondered whether the talent knew how those strings got pulled. My guess is that they knew enough to decide that they didn't always want to know everything.

George never did the work of booking someone himself. Sam Bramson, who was the head of the nightclub department, put in the booking slips, and then the list would be updated. That's how it worked. Someone else took care of the boring details. George didn't want people to know that, and he kept the information to himself, like compartments he was careful to seal. I was a compartment. I kept George's secrets and handled his money. I may have been paid by the William Morris Agency, but I *worked* for George.

George also worked for George. He lost a lot of money, and it made his life chaotic. He'd bet on anything. *How fast will that light change? How long will it take us to cross the street?* These wagers, no matter how small, served as his dopamine high.

Mostly, though, George bet on the fights. He was at heart a degenerate gambler. And, as is so often the case with heavy gamblers, George was also a prodigious spender. Money simply wouldn't stick to him, and he helped it fly. One day he called me into his office. He needed to buy a tie. "Go over to Sulka," he said. "Here's a couple hundred. Get me about six ties."

"What colors do you want?" I said.

"Do you see how I dress? Blue ties."

"All blue?"

"*Blue ties*," he snarled. So I went to Sulka on Madison Avenue and I bought him six blue ties in six different patterns. Does anyone *need* six blue ties?

George's immense appetites cut across all departments. Nothing was done on a small scale except his actual job. He used to get his shirts made at Sy's. All the guys had their shirts made at Sy's. They even sent their shirts there to be cleaned. Sy's shirts were delicate, the summer cuts made from cottons so thin they were almost transparent. They were the finest shirts, and his were always monogrammed: G.W.

Spending and gambling were George's addictions. They would be his undoing, and he wanted me to help him do both. The shirts and ties were beautiful, though—I had to give him that.

When I started working with George, I was young and nervous. I wanted to succeed in business without really trying, and I wasn't really trying. I would only push up to a point. My unwillingness to push made me amenable to doing George's bidding, no matter the request. It kept me from pushing back when Harry Kalcheim took credit for Bill Cosby and Barbra Streisand. Overall, it was a failure of my career.

But while I may not have been sure how to push enough to get ahead in the business, I did know one thing: it would be in my best interest to make sure George was dependent on me. How could I do that, though, when I was Murray Schwartz from the Bronx, and he was the legendary George Wood? Easy: money. I soon learned that it was through his finances that I could keep him safe—and simultaneously protect myself.

Don't get me wrong, George worried about money—*constantly*, in fact—and when he was losing it, that fear made him mean and volatile. But that didn't mean he did anything about it.

He failed to keep an eye on his balances or pay his debts. George made $500 a week, which would be like earning $5,000 a week today. And yet he was always broke. It was common for him to run to Chase Manhattan Bank to cover a check at the last minute. George, who was so adept at spending money, also seemed to fear it, so I simply stepped in.

Eventually, I started "kiting" checks for him, taking advantage of the three- or four-day period it took for a check to clear. I learned to cover his checks and managed the "float." This got me into some trouble with the IRS. Here I was, earning $40 a week, and suddenly thousands of dollars were washing through my little bank account. Eventually I started dating the teller at the bank. George liked that.

Looking back, I wonder why I didn't go into bookkeeping. After working for George, I could have become an accountant. Actually, I *was* an accountant—I was George's accountant.

Adding to this toxic brew was George's vanity. Late in life, he had his nose fixed. He must have been in his late fifties or early sixties, because I never knew him with his old nose. I think, like everything else in George's life, the decision was the result of a lost bet.

From time to time he'd ask for my opinion on a new purchase. "Does this suit fit me good?" he'd ask.

"Yes," I'd respond, "it does."

"You sure?" he'd ask. "You're not just saying that, right?"

"I'm sure, Mr. Wood," I'd say.

But I wasn't an ass-kisser, and I think he could see that from the start. It wasn't necessary for me to become sycophantic toward George, and I never said anything I didn't mean. Other times, he'd ask me which outfit I liked better. It was always a choice between two virtually identical blue suits. There's something reassuring about consistency. We admire people who know who they are. George may have had many problems, but he also knew who he was. His character was unwavering.

I, on the other hand, was as impressionable as wet cement.

CHAPTER 5

"Five-by-Seven or Eight-by-Ten?"

My world was becoming more and more incongruous. I was still living at home in the Bronx, but I was changing. The life I'd become familiar with growing up was utterly unlike the life in which I suddenly found myself. For example, the first time I went out to a high-level business dinner with George, I was stunned by the table settings. I'd never seen so many glasses lined up in my life. "White or red?" the waiter asked, and I didn't know how to answer.

"He'll have red," George responded, after a beat too long.

"What glass do I use?" I asked George, clearly fumbling in my new surroundings.

"Just do everything I do," said George. "Don't do nothing. Do what *I* do."

"You know what to do?"

"What the *fuck* do you take me for?" You couldn't question George.

Once, I called him by his name at a dinner with some of the boys. "That was funny, George," I said.

His response was like something out of *Goodfellas*. "What did you call me?" he growled.

"Me?" I said.

"You. What'd you call me?"

"What do you mean?"

"You didn't call me *George*, did you?"

"No, no." I was petrified.

And then everyone broke up laughing. I was being put on. Classic George.

I was learning a great deal from him—how the business worked, how to negotiate and read complex agreements. You know, the stuff they didn't teach in business school. I was also learning about elegance and style. As time went on, my rough edges were filed away. I picked up cues on how to dress, observing the details that made George impressive. His custom-made shirts, which came only with French cuffs, that "G.W." monogram embroidered into every one of them. I liked dressing like George too. At the time, I was a little too young for that look, but it stuck. To this day, I only wear custom monogrammed shirts with French cuffs.

It seems to me now that men of that era always seemed a little older than they actually were. I don't mean they seemed worn or tired. What I'm talking about is the fact that back then, men dressed like adults. And as such, they carried themselves that way—like adults.

Through clothing, men gave themselves an air of authority. This quality may seem to come with age, but I think it actually comes with self-respect and the acceptance of grown-up responsibilities. Even in this age of casual attire, the late-night talk show hosts are all suited up and well groomed.

In those days, people entered fully into adulthood, and they did it early. Men would never wear T-shirts and backward baseball caps to do anything other than mow the lawn. They cut their hair and shaved on a regular basis, and like George, they had their nails done. I still get my hair cut every ten days, so that it's always clean but never looks freshly cut. It's a part of my routine, a regular investment I make in myself.

But I didn't always have the dough to make those kinds of investments. Lucky for me, I got a little help bridging the gap between Bronx kid and burgeoning sophisticate.

Abe Lastfogel ran the William Morris Agency, and he and his wife, Frances, lived at the Essex House on Central Park South. Pretty early on, I was sent there to deliver a package. As I stepped into the lobby, I smelled flowers—tuberose, I believe. The scent was sweet and fresh and impressed upon me that this was the way those with money lived. Those flowers smelled like elegance.

Frances was kind of a Sophie Tucker type, big, and loud, and she was starting to like me. I was moving up the ladder a little and didn't have much in the way of clothes, and Frances took notice. One day, she told me to meet her at the Essex House.

"Sure. I'd be very happy to, but why?" I asked her.

"I want to give you some of the mister's suits," she said. With Mrs. Lastfogel, it was never "Abe." It was always "the mister."

"Oh, Mrs. Lastfogel, I think he's even a little shorter than *I* am."

"No, you're about the same size. You'll get the cuffs fixed. Don't worry about it."

When I arrived, she produced several of Abe Lastfogel's gorgeous custom-made suits and a stack of his shirts. I guess he didn't want them anymore. "See if these fit," she said. I checked the label of one of the shirts. Sy's. George had told Abe where to get his shirts made.

"I will, Mrs. Lastfogel. I'll take them home," I said.

"See if they fit here," she said.

"What do you want me to do?"

"Take your pants off. I've seen it before."

"What if Mr. Lastfogel walks in? I'd hate to be standing in your apartment in my underwear."

"Don't worry about it. He'll know I'm giving you his clothes. Don't make a fuss about it."

I was a little boy to Frances Lastfogel, and she wanted me to look nice. She and Abe were so in love. They were totally devoted to each other, but they'd never had children. Maybe she was trying to expend a little of that maternal energy on me. So I tried the clothes on right there at her request. She appraised me and considered me fit for service, and I took them home.

"Now, don't tell everybody," she said as she sent me on my way.

Not long after that, I was sitting in a TV department meeting, way in the back of the room, and feeling like a real big shot. My legs were crossed, ankle to knee. I was leaning over, my arm resting on them, and my jacket was open. Just then, a buddy pointed to the inside of my jacket.

"What's your problem?" I said. Then I realized: the letters *A.L.* were stitched inside the jacket. The monogram was visible. I closed the jacket and buttoned it.

Whether or not Abe Lastfogel's suits helped me advance, I was making progress. I had become involved with commercials and started working with Fred Allen, who was a big star at the time. Checks would come through, we'd take our commission, and then they'd go on to Fred.

One day, a check came in for him—for only $100. I thought I was Mr. Big Shot, Murray Schwartz, who now had a secretary and everything. *My God,* I thought, *the guy's getting checks for a million dollars a year. What's the point of charging commission on a little $100 check?* So I told my secretary, "Oh, just send that to accounting. No commission."

Well, it got to Mr. Lastfogel that I'd done that. He didn't call me to his office, which still fascinates me to this day. Instead, he walked right into mine and sat down.

"Yes, sir?" I said, standing.

"Sit down, sit down," he said. "You can sit." I continued standing.

"Is there anything I can do for you, Mr. Lastfogel? Would you like some coffee?"

"I don't drink coffee," he said. Then, "Did you send that check to Fred Allen without taking commission?"

"I did," I said. "I thought it would be a very nice gesture to show Mr. Allen that we care about him."

"*Nice?* You know how stupid that was?"

"Gee, I really don't, sir," I said. I was being very respectful.

"Do you know the policy here? What is our policy?" asked Mr. Lastfogel.

"You want me to quote it?"

"Yeah, I want you to quote it. It's not a long policy. Let me hear you say it."

"Well," I said, "we get 10 percent commission—"

"—on *everything*," he said. "Now, if you don't take it on the $100, he's gonna call me and say, 'Why are you taking it on $100,000?'"

Then he looked around my office. I'd been allowed to design it myself, and it was pretty chic, if I do say so—I had acquired good taste hanging around George. I had a French writing desk and a Ralph Lauren–style plaid couch opposite it. On the wall, I had pictures of a couple of the stars we worked with.

Mr. Lastfogel said, "You have a very nice office. There's just one thing: get those goddamn pictures off the wall."

"But Mr. Lastfogel," I replied, "they're our clients."

"Yeah, and soon one client will come in and say, 'Why isn't my picture there? Why isn't mine higher than his?' Get them down. You can have your family up there, but I don't want your clients' pictures on the wall." It was an interesting insight.

We'd followed the same principle at the Red Mill. Our dressing rooms were numbered, but none of them were "Number One." My dad was smart enough to say, "Every stripper's gonna want that dressing room. Big or small inside, they don't care." So he said, "Put a star on the door of every room and begin with number fifteen."

Later on, I did the same thing at the Celebrity Theater we owned at Merv Griffin Enterprises. What worked at the Red Mill worked at William Morris, and later in my career. What if Sophia Loren and Ava Gardner were on the show the same night? There'd be hell to pay if one of them had to be in Dressing Room Number Two.

* * *

It's said that the olfactory sense has the most indelible memory. It's that way for everyone. Catch a whiff on the breeze, whether it's violets or floor wax, and suddenly you're transported through space and time. The lobby of the Essex House smelled like fresh flowers. The shirts and suits I took from Mrs. Lastfogel smelled of clean starch and carefully aired closets.

My memories of the Red Mill are as driven by smell as my memories of the fine life in Manhattan. But there was nothing fresh in the Bronx. Up in my old neighborhood, the memory-triggering smells were of cooking; french fries; beer, the musky; slightly sour smell of the bars; and the pervasive whiff of struggle. The Bronx smelled old, but it was old hopes I was sniffing, not old money.

I remember the smells of the Red Mill's kitchen, where I spent afternoons peeling potatoes and laughing with the cooks. The chef was famous for his roast chicken, but every so often the chickens we got were moldy, and we had to scrub the raw birds with a mixture of Clorox and water. The bleach would sting the inside of my nose as my dad and I scrubbed those chickens side by side. I thought it was hilarious, so much so that the scent of chlorine still makes me smile.

The basement was also one of my places. The beer was kept down there in kegs, so the smell of stale ale permeated the walls and floors. Supporting the ceiling were thick wooden beams. They seemed to be centuries old and gave the effect of a historic France in a space the customers never saw.

The basement was where the house photographer had her darkroom, where she developed the photos taken of the customers on their big nights out. Photos were an important moneymaker at the Red Mill. The photographer was a sexy woman in a low-cut dress, and she walked by the tables snapping pictures. Once they were developed, she'd present them in a fancy folder. "How many do you want?" she'd say. "Two? One for you and one for your friend? Five-by-seven or eight-by-ten?"

The customers loved them. For many, it was a rare night out, and to have a memento of themselves, dressed nattily in their finest suits and dresses, sitting proudly in front of a full table or dancing cheek to cheek was too good an offer to pass up.

That wasn't the only value-add we offered—the Mill also sold personalized matchbooks. "Your photo on a matchbook cover, while you wait," the photographer would offer with a smile. While she sold her wares, I was in the darkroom, developing the pictures. I got to love photography working there.

I learned how to make the matchbooks too. We'd print the picture on half-cut sheets of photo paper; on the other half was a sketch of the Red Mill. Then we'd fold the paper around a blank white matchbook, so that the customer's image was on one side and the Mill was on the other. Add a striking edge, and voilà—the matchbook was complete. I can still smell the sharp, sulfuric smoke of those struck matches, and I can see the glow of faces turning bright for that brief moment while a cigarette was lit. Then the match would go out, and the faces would return to shadow.

CHAPTER 6

"Another Round of the Egg Salad"

've been asked about the nature of my relationship with George. What was the dynamic? Well, it wasn't father and son, which perhaps is what people were getting at when they asked me that question. It was boss and assistant, period. On that, there was never any confusion.

I worked for George for two and a half years. Nobody lasted with him as long as I did. Other guys would hold out for a few weeks, maybe a few months at most. George was scary. He was intimidating, moody, and hard to get along with. He frightened people, yelling at them all the time, and I certainly never heard him tell a joke. He swore constantly. I have to use the word *fuck* when I talk about George, because with him, it was always "fuck this" and "fuck that."

He never uttered a four-letter word in front of a woman, though. In fact, even George fell in love—and when he did, it was immediate. In a twist of fate, I met George's future wife before he did. Lois was a talented singer and actress, an effortlessly beautiful blonde. She had been Florence Henderson's understudy for the traveling company of *Oklahoma!*

Lois and George were introduced in 1959 by Jimmy Van Heusen, one of the greatest songwriters this country has ever produced and a four-time Oscar winner. Lois came up to the office one day, looking for George on Van Heusen's recommendation. George was out, so I greeted her. After apologizing that George wasn't there to meet her, I called him to ask what he'd like me to say to her.

"What's she look like?" George said.

"Just like Grace Kelly," I said, which was true.

"What's she wearing?"

"A dress with flowers on it," I said.

"Oh, brother," said George. "Ask her to have cocktails with me, then take her to Best and Co. and buy her a black dress and pearls." He liked women in black dresses and "poils."

So I took Lois shopping and charged the dress and necklace to George's account. Later that evening, George and Lois met for the first time and fell in love instantly. A few months later he married her. They had two daughters, and Lois left show business to raise her family. Years after George died, she married Generoso Pope Jr., the owner of the *National Enquirer*.

* * *

George certainly wasn't as kind to me as he was to Lois during their courtship—why would he be? She was his girlfriend. But because we worked so closely, there were times when he couldn't help but show me his softer side. It was something few others got to see.

One time he was working from home, and he called me over to help. The weather was nasty—a storm was raging outside—and I

through many hard moments with George. I often didn't like what he did, but in my wide-eyed, youthful state, I didn't react.

* * *

As I explained earlier, George served a different purpose than the other agents at William Morris. The agency represented the biggest names in show business, and here was George, mixing with a rogues' gallery of goodfellas.

Jimmy Blue Eyes was mob royalty. Jimmy worked with Meyer Lansky, to whom he was introduced by Lucky Luciano. Jimmy was a capo in the Genovese crime family and looked just like Robert De Niro—which is perfect, of course, given that De Niro's *American Hustle* character, Victor Tellegio, is partly based on Jimmy Alo.

I really liked Jimmy. I knew what he was and what he was up to, but there was something very charming about him. He was intelligent, thoughtful, and an avid reader. In fact, all of the boys liked to read. They were always sharp and contemporary, more like businessmen than mobsters. The image of a crime figure living and lurking in the shadows is false. These guys were in the center of it all, out at shows, shaking hands, reading the latest books, up on the most important current events, and always at the forefront of fashion.

What I remember is Jimmy's smile. He wanted to become a legitimate businessman, but the guys at the agency didn't like "Jimmy Blue Eyes" hanging around. So when he came to see George, he had to be whisked inside to George's inner office. George would alert me that Jimmy was on his way up.

"Don't wait in here," he'd say to me. "You wait outside, in the reception area, and you walk him right in. I don't want Jimmy sitting out there. When he arrives, you're *right* there. You walk him in, and you open this door for him."

"Who's gonna answer your phone?" I asked.

"I'll answer the fuckin' phone. You just take care of Jimmy B."

George was in everything. He told me that the singer Vic Damone had knocked up the daughter of one of the guys, and they planned to throw Damone off of a fire escape. He relished telling me the story: "I got a phone call, and I went over there and hauled him back in through the window."

Nonetheless, George was disliked, a gambler whose life ended mysteriously and whose career amounted to mostly back-alley business. It may have been nicely dressed back-alley business, but it was underhanded and negotiated with threats.

There was value in it, though. The mob has a credo, and it doesn't forget who its friends are. I think I got along with Jimmy and the others because of my boyhood at the Red Mill. After a while, it was clear I was their favorite. I accepted the culture and knew not to push them. That knowledge was my entrée to a better world. Jimmy knew me when I was George Wood's secretary. He knew me to be honest, he respected my loyalty, and he remembered how careful I'd been with George's finances. These guys respected money, and they respected those who knew how to handle it.

At one point, Jimmy B. offered to set me up in my own management firm. "Do what you want to do," George said. "But I'm warning you that you're going to have a lot of partners within a week."

The mob was the mob, and being close to it meant dancing with real danger. One afternoon I was coming out of the subway station just below the Park Sheraton Hotel. I was on my way back to the Morris office after running an errand for George. The Park Sheraton was near our building, and I passed it all the time—but this time was different. I found myself caught in a large crowd. Something big was going on.

From the sidewalk near the entrance to the subway station, I could see into the window of the hotel's barbershop. There, on the floor, was a body. It was partly covered with blood-soaked towels.

When I finally got to George's office, I asked him if he knew what had happened. "What are you talking about, kid?" he said, sounding bored and uninterested.

"Albert Anastasia just got shot downstairs," I said. Albert Anastasia, one of the most ruthless members of Cosa Nostra, a founder of the American Mafia, and the head of Murder Incorporated, had been gunned down in the hotel. "They shot him right down there, in the *barbershop.*"

"What time is it?" asked George. I told him, and he slowly looked at his watch. After a second or two, he nodded. "Yeah, that's about right." George acted as though he knew the hit was going to happen, and precisely at what time.

"Did you see it?" George asked.

"I saw *him* lying on the floor, covered in towels."

Later, I learned that George didn't know when the hit was to take place, or that it had even been ordered. But it was in keeping with his persona to behave as if he were also a mobster.

* * *

There are many rumors about George's death, most of them centered on a possible mob connection. One thing I do know is that it didn't have anything to do with William Morris, or any deal between the mob and the agency. The heads of William Morris would never allow the *Mafia* to buy into the company. Lastfogel and the others didn't even like Jimmy Blue Eyes showing up at the office. But Jimmy would meet George almost daily at around 5 p.m., just before cocktails. Some days, Jimmy would come up to the office, unshaven and wearing a leather jacket with suit pants. It was a strange getup. Then George and Jimmy would go together for hot shaves and shoe shines. Sometimes they'd also get haircuts.

I used to think that I could have gone that way, into organized crime. After all, I was offered the chance and could easily have taken it. I still think about why I didn't. These guys intrigued me, and their lifestyle had a surface appeal.

But ultimately, I saw that the romance of organized crime is paper thin and the reality brutal, and choosing that life was usually no choice at all. George's main characteristic was desperation. I watched him, and I saw how hard he made things for himself. I decided early to take from him only that which would serve me. Fineness, beauty, art, elegance—those were worth holding onto. Phone calls from the boys, I could leave those behind.

* * *

One of the perks of working at William Morris was the arrival each morning of a coffee cart from Schrafft's, the famous New York restaurant chain known largely for its ladies lunches, candies, and ice cream. The cart would roll down the office hallways laden with the loveliest cakes and pastries, pots of fresh, hot coffee, and little jugs of cream. We'd hear the cart coming down the hall and flock into the hallway for our midmorning coffee break.

You don't see touches like that in business anymore. It was charming. These days, we have our bland paper cups from Starbucks. When the Schrafft's cart came, we didn't have to leave the office, which made the practice efficient, but mostly it was a nicety that made our days feel a little more special, a tiny touch of glamour with our cup of coffee.

One day I was sitting at my desk when George looked up and said, "What the fuck is that noise?" A rattling, growing louder as it approached.

"That's Schrafft's," I said. George had a fondness for their delicate egg salad sandwiches. It was always funny to me that tough guys like Jimmy Blue Eyes, Sugar Brown, Champ Segal, and George liked to eat at ladies tearooms like Schrafft's and Rumplemayer's. Rumplemayer's was on Central Park South, next to the St. Moritz Hotel and George's apartment building at 40 Central Park South. There, the group of hardened mobsters would eat egg salad and cucumber tea sandwiches on thin slices of white bread, cut into tiny triangles and served on doilies. They would pick up these little triangles and hold them carefully between their thick fingers. The sandwiches would be followed by lacy tea cookies that arrived on tiered plates. They ordered vanilla milkshakes served in tall, curved soda fountain glasses. "Dey got any more ah dese sandwiches?" they'd say. We'd wave at the waitresses. "Hey, sweetheart! Another rounda' the egg salad. And what's that other one? Watercress. Dose too."

Then it was back to business. "Did you see that fucking horse?"

It was an absurd scene. The boys' favorite subjects were gambling and unpaid debts, and they didn't see the need to clean up their act to make nice with Central Park South. Ladies who lunched in little hats would look over at our table with a mixture of disgust and fear.

One day the Schrafft's coffee cart arrived outside of our office like it always did. George said, "Come on, kid, let's get something." George got a piece of cake, and I ordered coffee and a doughnut. George turned to leave, and the Schrafft's lady said, "Hey, *mista!*"

OK, here we go, I thought.

"You talking to me?" George said gruffly. He actually said, à la the movie *Taxi Driver*, "You talkin' to me? What's your problem?"

"You didn't pay," said the lady from Schrafft's. She was Irish, and no pushover. George shot me a pissed-off look.

"Take care of it," he said. I realized he meant for me to pay out of my own pocket. I hesitated. "Well, take *care* of it," he said. The underpaid secretary is invited to get coffee and is *commanded* to pay? What was I going to say, though? *No?* I paid the woman and thought, *What a shit.*

Years later, when I was running Merv Griffin Enterprises, I provided coffee and pastries for everyone in the morning. Merv said, "Murray, that's a huge waste of money, isn't it?"

"No, it isn't," I said. "Take a look around. No one's leaving the office." That was another thing I learned from George: the importance of true loyalty and generosity. It was one of those lessons you learn from being shown how *not* to do something.

* * *

George was motivated by self-interest. As long as I fulfilled his needs, he would allow me to continue fulfilling them. With George there was no exchange. I don't think George could be loyal to anybody. One could never be sure which side of the street George was working. As my experience with Sugar Brown ought to have taught me, George wasn't above selling out his best friends. But he couldn't test his tough-guy buddies the way he could test me. In that equation, the power was tipped toward the boys. When it came to other people, though, George treated them like disposable commodities.

Women were equally at risk of experiencing George's utilitarian approach to relationships. He had a very active casting couch.

By this time I had my own private cubicle, with a door and a file cabinet. The only thing of George's in my office was a coat stand. Every day he'd walk in and say, "Good morning, kid" (it was always "kid"; I'd been promoted from "Sonny" to "kid"), and he'd take off his hat and flick it onto the coat stand. I'm still impressed he could do that. Then he'd take off his coat and hand it to me, and I'd hang it up. (By then I was thinking for myself, and I didn't like his hat and coat in my private office, but I wasn't about to tell *him* that.)

We communicated primarily through an intercom system, but he often asked me to turn the intercom off so I didn't hear what was going on. Occasionally, though, I did turn it on, to get a little insight into all that was happening on that casting couch.

No matter how much I admired George's surface appearance, I didn't respect him. I didn't want to follow too closely in his footsteps. When I got to be more successful, I learned to play blackjack like a pro—just like George did. I dressed like him too. I saw myself as a young George Wood, doing it all over again—the dames, the tables, and the tough guys. But when I felt like I began enjoying gambling a little too much, I stopped and went to Gamblers Anonymous. I knew better, and I got help. It saved me from making an awful mess of things.

CHAPTER 7

"Remember When We Almost Went to Jail Together?"

I've always been responsible—maybe a little too responsible. I was somewhat of a playboy, sure, but that mentality never spilled over into the rest of my life. There aren't mirrors on the ceiling at my house. Instead, I have an elegant cottage with roses and fireplaces, a place where I can hang out with my golden retriever, Valentina. I was born an old soul, and that has always been reflected in my behavior.

Even though I was responsible, I still got into jams. I wasn't Mr. Goody Two Shoes; I'd had the chutzpah to go up to the Morris office and con my way into a job. I'd schmooze around; I knew how to play—and this came in handy when I was drafted.

Remember, the draft didn't stop after WWII. It was peacetime, but guys were still going into the army, and once drafted, they had to stay for two years of active duty. But there was another option: a program in which one could serve full-time for six months and then become a member of the reserves for fifteen or twenty years. It was a ridiculous amount of time to be in the reserves, but I didn't want to lose my job with George, and I thought there was a chance he'd hold my position for me if I only had to be gone for six months. So I presented the six-month option to him as a unique opportunity. If he agreed, I could fulfill my duty and be back at my desk in half a year.

"Will you give me time off?" I asked. I was astounded when he said yes. He could have filled that position a hundred times over. Holding it for me was a pretty magnanimous thing to do, more proof that he really did like me after all. Now I just had to figure out how to get into the program, since there was a long list of guys who wanted in.

I had a connection to Mario Puzo, who was working for the Army administration, signing people up for the six-month program. Mario was a writer—he'd just written *The Dark Arena*, and he would go on to write one of the greatest American novels, *The Godfather*—but lots of people need a day job when they're just starting out.

Jerry Tokofsky, my mailroom buddy, knew Mario . . . and he also knew about a little side hustle that Mario had. For a hundred bucks—under the table, of course—Mario would let you cut the line, getting you in ahead of everyone else. My place in the program wouldn't quite be legit, but I'd be able to keep my job.

George gave me that $100 to give to Mario, and I was in. Six months later, when I got out of the army, I brought Mario into the William Morris Agency to write more books, and he wrote *The Godfather*. To me, Mario Puzo is in the same category as John Steinbeck. I have a signed copy of *The Godfather* in which he wrote, "Do you remember when we almost went to jail together?" Though no one had ever threatened to put us in jail, what we had done was definitely illegal, and it became a running joke.

While in the army, I earned a sharpshooting medal. I'd never held a rifle before, but as it turned out, I had pretty good aim.

When my service in Fort Dix, New Jersey, was up, I went to the office to visit George dressed in my uniform, with the funny little hat and tan pants and my sharpshooting medal pinned to my chest. He had everyone come in to see me. Looking at my medal, he said, "What's that? You win an award?"

"Sharpshooter," I said. That pleased George immensely.

George called Jimmy Blue Eyes. "Jimmy, guess what? The kid's gonna be helpful to you later." It was all a joke, of course.

* * *

Working with George wasn't all rough guys and threats, cursing, and blood-spattered floors. There were some nice times, too. My facility with contracts meant that I got as close to the performers as one could. Sammy Davis Jr. was staying at the Gorham Hotel, two blocks from Carnegie Hall, and George asked me to go up to his room and get Sammy to sign a big contract.

"Sure, Mr. Wood," I said, and I sailed out of the office. This was going to be fun. Sammy had a reputation for being a little difficult, but also for being a one-man party.

The Gorham was a small hotel. Because Sammy was black, he wasn't able to stay in hotels that were of a stature commensurate with his fame—blacks weren't welcome at the Plaza in those days. Even when he headlined at the Copacabana, he had to enter through the *kitchen*, while Frank, Dino, Joey, and the other stars entered through the front door.

When I arrived at Sammy's apartment at the Gorham, dressed in my nice suit, Sammy himself opened the door. His hair was pressed against his head in a women's stocking. I'd never seen anyone with

83

a stocking on his head before, and I couldn't help but stare at it. He said, "What the fuck are you staring at?"

"Nothing, Mr. Davis," I sputtered. "I'm sorry. I have a contract for you to look at."

He agreed to look at it, but first he offered me a drink. Soon we became just two guys having a whiskey. Jack Daniels—two fingers, one rock. He showed me how he put Vaseline in his hair to straighten it.

Eventually, Sammy started smoking grass. Then George called. "Is he doing it? Is he signing it?" he asked.

"Yeah, he is," I said. "We're just going to hang out a little bit more."

"If you don't get that contract signed, don't come back," George snarled into the phone.

Great. George in hardball mode. But Sammy was a very nice guy, and he signed the contract so that we could put work aside and relax. We were friends after that. With Sammy, it was always, "OK, kid." Sammy offered me a joint, and as I sat there smoking grass with this big star, I thought, *This is a great job*.

Years later, I ended up living in the same building as Sammy: 370 East 76th Street. He lived on a higher floor, and his mother, Elvera, lived on my floor. I had just married Ann, and we'd just had our first child, Suzy. Elvera would often babysit for us.

At the time, Sammy was married to the Swedish movie actress May Britt. Their marriage in November 1960 was highly controversial, as interracial marriage was still illegal in many states. The big rumor was that JFK and Bobby Kennedy had told Frank Sinatra to ask Sammy to postpone the wedding until after the 1960 presidential election. Maybe it was a coincidence, but he did postpone the wedding.

Before that, Sammy was dating the actress Kim Novak. It made the boys edgy because the relationship threatened to ice her career. I know that George made a call because I heard him on the phone. Sammy suddenly married a black Vegas showgirl. (Their relationship was short lived.)

George certainly had a lot of power in some circles.

* * *

By the time I lived in the same apartment as the Davises, my career was taking off, and my digs were indicative of that. Joe Namath and many other famous stars lived in our building too. There was a pool on the roof—we never knew whether we were getting a suntan or whether it was just the New York City soot settling on our skin. It was a beautiful building, and it's still there, as lovely as ever.

Why did I still care deeply about glamour at that stage of my life? After all, by then I had lived with it for a number of years and seen that glamour could have a sinister side, too. When I mull it over, I keep coming back to the Red Mill. We're shaped by our past, and our first desires propel us throughout our lives. The Red Mill was the glamour in the Bronx; it was special, and it made *me* feel special. Everyone in the neighborhood was trying so hard to meet the people at the Red Mill, and here I was, surrounded by them. I was one of them.

It wasn't easy to gain entrée into that world, but I was born into it, a prince in a kingdom of the Bronx. It wasn't a charmed life, but I know now that it was rare. I inhaled different oxygen than the other kids. It was smokier air that I breathed, and it smelled of whiskey and rye, and of the powder on the dancers. It was part of my DNA, and I loved it. My skin absorbed the Red Mill; I metabolized it like sugar, and it fueled my quest for a better life. That's why the Red Mill has stayed with me all these years.

George worked hard to conceal his money troubles and the down-and-dirty facts of his life. Perhaps that was why he pursued glamour so aggressively, and why I made a conscious decision at the Red Mill to pursue it too. Maybe George and I were a good match in the short term because we recognized in each other the need to survive the hardships of life, and we found solace in the same things. Glamour carried me over the rough waves. Flowers, fine suits, custom shirts, and well-made things nourished me. They still do.

To this day, thanks to George's influence and my memories of the Red Mill, bouquets of fresh flowers are placed throughout my house. There are no photos of the Red Mill in the Bronx, but I have an oil painting of its namesake, the Moulin Rouge. The two windmills are alike enough that the picture has come to mean "The Red Mill" to me, and it reminds me of where I began.

Below the glamorous surface of my fancy apartment building, however, my life was more difficult than it appeared. It was the core values instilled in me by my dad—personal responsibility, moral clarity, and a strong refusal to be beaten down—that kept me moving forward toward the life I wanted. He really did me a great service by hauling me out of Percy's Pool Room and into the Red Mill.

CHAPTER 8

A Million Watts of Neon

For a boy who grew up among the showgirls, club waiters, and petty wise guys of the Red Mill, there was one place with a draw equal to that of Midtown Manhattan: Las Vegas. Talk about glamour. Vegas in the 1970s burned like the Red Mill lit by a million watts of neon.

My introduction to Las Vegas was through George. George loved gambling the way flower beds love rain. For George, though, the rain didn't fall nearly often enough. Nevertheless, a large part of George's success was due to his connections in Vegas. The network he'd built across the US and Europe made him valuable to people who needed things done, but George's clout in Vegas was the most important connection of all.

Vegas was crucial to celebrities—every big name played there. At William Morris, a guy named Wallace Jordan headed the TV department. Jordan was connected to the advertising agencies. He was sharp, and he looked the part. William Morris was smart in that regard: they knew how to cast their agents for their parts.

It seems unbelievable today, but in those days the big advertising agencies were not, shall we say, inclined to hire Jews. It was well known, and part of the reason I went to William Morris. The so-called Jewish Mafia of the entertainment business didn't rise up out of a desire to keep others out, or to hoard power. It was simply the way business worked back then. We went where we could excel, get promoted, and use our skills to their highest potential. Things have changed since I was young, but it's nice to feel a sense of belonging. It wasn't easy to get, and as with many young, ambitious men of my generation, belonging was important to me. We understood the value of clubs, even unofficial clubs. In Los Angeles, the Hillcrest Country Club south of Beverly Hills was opened in 1920 exclusively for Jewish members. It soon became the home of the powerful Hollywood elite, which included the big guys from the William Morris Agency.

Vegas was a club too—the biggest club at the time. It still is, though I miss the glamour of the Rat Pack, and the style and wit of Frank, Dean, and Sammy. It was so much fun when I was there. Whenever we were filming *The Merv Griffin Show* at Caesars Palace, I had my own suite there. And when we weren't, they were so gracious, comping RFB (room, food, and beverage) anytime I was there. Here I was, a guy who'd come from living in a Bronx walk-up to having his own suite at Caesars, sleeping in a bed shaped like an oyster with a Jacuzzi in the floor next to him!

But back when I was working for George, we would stay at the Riviera. One time, George decided to teach me how to play blackjack. I was a novice, but I had the anchor seat, and I made a classic rookie mistake: I split tens. The game is Twenty-One: You do *not* split tens. I busted, which meant I busted George's hand, and the dealer broke everybody. I thought, *I better get outta here*. I walked into the Riviera's brightly tiled men's room and stood at a long row of urinals in my dark wool suit. The room was so stark it could have been filmed in color and it still would have looked like black and white.

That was a stupid move, I thought. I didn't have to think it twice, though, because George stormed in a few seconds after me, screaming. George was a screamer at the best of times—and busting a hand was the worst of times.

"Fuckin' son of a fuckin' bitch!" George was blasting, his face red, the veins on his neck standing out purple. The black-and-white scene in the men's room was now in Technicolor. There were over a dozen available urinals, and George took the one next to me and unzipped his fly. We were alone except for the shoeshine guy at the far end. George continued to scream at me, curses coming out of his mouth in a jet. He was really losing his mind; he was on anger autopilot: "How stupid are you? How the fuck could you do that?" Because he was in a blind rage, possessed by demonic fury, he didn't notice he'd turned toward me while using the urinal . . . and as he yelled, facing me, he pissed on my pants. Just like that, right on my leg.

That was it. I quit.

"Fuck *you*!" I said. "I've taken your shit for too long. Go fuck yourself. I know tough guys too, and I'm quitting. I'm leaving." I booked the first flight back to New York and went to my room to pack.

A few minutes before I was to leave the room, there was a knock on the door. I opened it, and standing in the hallway was a delivery person from Sy Devore, the famous men's clothier, holding a suit carrier. In it was a beautiful blue suit. It was from George. There was no apology, just the blue suit. A little later, he called.

"Are you still quitting?"

"No."

The truth is, George didn't mean to piss on my pants. He'd simply lost control, a captive of his gambling addiction and whatever lay underneath it. But it was my best blue wool suit he'd peed on, and I didn't have a lot of clothes. In fact, my suit had come from Sy Devore originally, so it was nice that the replacement was also from Sy's.

In another twist, many years later Merv and I ended up owning the building in Los Angeles where Sy Devore has his store. It's moved from the original Hollywood location to a spot not far from my house, and sometimes, when I pass it, I remember George screaming at me and then trying to make it better with a blue suit.

Working in Vegas wasn't always that dramatic, but it was consistently colorful. After all, people don't go to Vegas to behave. Long before the city's tagline "What happens in Vegas stays in Vegas" became a common expression, that was how we all "did" Vegas. For example, one form of etiquette one learned early on was that one didn't "send over" a hooker. You were to choose your own. So George's buddy would say to me, "Hey, Murray, I want you to meet my friend. Her father's from Switzerland; he's a famous clockmaker." Then he'd turn to the girl and say, "Honey, would you take Mr. Schwartz upstairs and fix his clock for him?" It was a crude world.

Maybe some other guys would have sent me a hooker to make up for peeing on my leg, but that wasn't George's style. The suit was his style. He respected clothes as much as he respected people. Scratch that: George respected clothes *more* than he respected people.

In Vegas, then as now, everything was inverted. Day was night and night was day. That's why you never see clocks in the casino. When I was running Merv Griffin Enterprise, I was told to have a meeting at one o'clock with Jerry Zarowitz, who ran Caesars, to negotiate a deal to bring *The Merv Griffin Show* to Vegas. When I arrived at his office, coming out of the bright Vegas afternoon into the artificial night of the casino, his secretary looked at me strangely.

"I'm here for my meeting with Mr. Zarowitz," I said.

"He's not here," she said.

"Oh, I'm sorry," I said. "He told me to meet him at one o'clock."

"*In the morning*," she said.

How the hell was I supposed to know that?

The guys at Caesars Palace often negotiated at night. They usually started around five o' clock, before going to dinner. And they drank—heavily. I couldn't keep up with them, so George taught me a trick. I'd arrive early, slip the waiter or bartender some cash, and say that when I nodded and ordered a Johnnie Walker Black—that's what I would drink with the guys—to make it an apple cider. I always tipped $50; they were taking a risk doing that, and I was always grateful. I'd have a couple of real ones and then I'd nod. After that, the pour was apple cider on the rocks. An apple cider on the rocks looks just like scotch, and it tastes sweet and nice. That's how I could stay with the boys and not lose my focus or my edge.

"You having another one?" The question always came.

"Yeah, I'm having another one," I'd say, and the bartender would smile.

Just like the sign Sam had framed in the pee house at the Red Mill, "Keep your eye upon the doughnut and not upon the hole." The deals are the doughnut, and I had to make the best deals I could. But I was there with the tough guys—you knew it would work out in their best interests. The house always wins.

Still, I was grateful for the early exposure to Vegas, a gift from George. That experience helped me negotiate that 1 a.m. deal to bring *The Merv Griffin Show* there, making it the first national television show to be broadcast from that city. The show originated from Caesars Palace for ten weeks a year for the next fifteen years. But more on that later.

We also produced a number of other shows at Caesars, including the first all-black show. It was called *Isaac Hayes*, and it starred Isaac Hayes himself, plus B.B. King and many others. We did Paul Anka's special too: Wayne Newton was a special guest, along with some Argentinean gauchos. I showed the bosses at Caesars that the kind of promotion we gave them—with our show broadcasting from their theater during the day, when it was idle anyway—was unparalleled. The resulting revenue on the slots became a major daytime source of income for them, and they paid us a hefty fee in return.

Several years later, Merv and I were in Monte Carlo to head up a tennis tournament to raise money for the Princess Grace Foundation, a charity founded in honor of Princess Grace of Monaco by her husband, Prince Rainier. Merv was Princess Grace's dinner companion, and I escorted Princess Antoinette, Prince Rainier's sister. While I was in Monte Carlo, I met Princess Antoinette's daughter, Christine de Massy, and we ended up dating for a while. Coincidentally, her father, who was a tennis pro, lived a few miles from me in Los Angeles. We'd visit him often. I cared deeply about her. She was smart, elegant, and understated, despite her background—an attribute that came from her mother, no doubt. She died young, and I was stunned by the loss.

Princess Antoinette was so impressed by my comfort with royal protocol that she asked if I'd been in the company of royalty often. Of course, we'd been briefed by the palace on what to do, but I had a few drinks in me, and I said I'd dated Princess Fatima of Caesars Palace for years. That got me one of the biggest laughs of my life.

(When cigarettes were sold in casinos, a voice would call over the loudspeaker, "Calling Princess Fatima," and a girl with a cigarette box would arrive at the tables wearing a short white-and-gold Greek goddess outfit.)

* * *

George's gift of the blue suit after he ruined mine may seem gracious, even given the offensive nature of the incident that precipitated it, but George himself wasn't gracious. In fact, he could be even less charming when he received a gift than when he gave one.

On one occasion George offered his apartment to Frank Sinatra to use to meet up with a woman. Thinking Frank had already left, George went home one afternoon a little early. He opened the door, and Frank said, "What do you want? What are you doing here?" George was so pissed off by Frank's attitude that they got into a shoving match in the hallway.

"Get outta here!" George said. Afterward, Frank realized that he *was* in George's apartment and perhaps should have been a little more grateful, so he sent George an Audemars Piguet watch to make up for it. They're gorgeous watches, very slim and elegant. George looked at the watch and said, "Take a letter to Frank Sinatra." Then he dictated, "Take this watch and stick it in your fuckin' ass."

"That's what you want me to type?" I said.

"Yeah, type it, and type *fuckin'*. Not 'fucking,' but 'F-U-C-K-I-N.' And sign it, 'Best wishes, George.' In fact, don't even put it in a box. Put it in a fuckin' envelope and put a stamp on it, and send it back to him." I did what George asked and sent the watch back with that letter to Frank Sinatra. I guess I could have kept the watch, but that letter was the funniest thing to me, and I laughed all the way to the mailroom.

A few years earlier, Sinatra's career had been on a downward spiral. George was close to Harry Cohn, the powerful chief of Columbia Pictures. George flew out to see him; it wasn't unlike what happens with Johnny Fontane in *The Godfather*. (In fact, the character of Fontane was based on Sinatra, although there was no horse head in a bed.) George was instrumental in getting Sinatra the role of Private Maggio in the film *From Here to Eternity*. Sinatra received the Academy Award for best supporting actor, and his career shot back up; he became greater than ever. Sadly, George never got the credit he deserved for being one of Frank's agents at William Morris—just as I never got credit for bringing stars to the agency earlier in my career.

Another time, as a thank you for a favor George did for Ed Sullivan, Ed sent George a new Mercury car. *The Ed Sullivan Show* was sponsored by Lincoln Mercury's dealers nationwide. George took that car straight to the dealer and sold it for cash. Sullivan called him and said, "How could you do that?"

"First of all, I don't drive," said George. "And second, if I did drive a car, I wouldn't drive a Mercury. I'd drive a Lincoln." I laughed hysterically at this. George said to me, "I might have driven the Lincoln. I'd have hired a driver to take me around in a Mercury." George could be horrible, but he could also truly make me laugh. In any case, George probably sold the Mercury because he needed gambling dough. Besides, a Mercury wasn't as nice as a Lincoln.

CHAPTER 9

"Three People Will Survive"

I never considered George a friend. But I did watch him, looking for cues. George's unscrupulousness didn't serve him well, and over time I came to see that it was a cheap, short-term answer that would pay poorly in the long run. Slowly, I realized, "This isn't a happy guy. He can't even afford these suits. He's a pawn." Admittedly, he was a high-level pawn, but that didn't change the fact that the boys paid him to do favors. He'd been my idol, and then one day I discovered he was a phony, an empty bag.

When George was up, he was really up. When things went his way, he was the greatest guy, especially when he won a bet. "Come on, we're going out to dinner," he'd say, and we'd go to Dinty Moore's on West 46th Street and have baby chickens. "Order chickens," George said. "Shall I order four? Don't you eat?" That was his way of inviting me.

But when he was losing, watch out. And eventually I got tired of watching out, of gauging his moods, guarding his secrets, and keeping my pants free of his piss. It was time to move on. I'd outlasted every other assistant he'd ever had and taken all I could. I felt I'd learned all I needed to learn from George.

But I couldn't get away that easily. I came to him and asked, "What's my next step?" He wasn't altruistic, but he knew that I was loyal, and that meant something. I knew how to keep things private. When his phone was being tapped, I knew not to call out from the office. This wasn't the sort of thing one could put on a résumé, but George understood its value: keep your friends close and your enemies closer. He made sure I stayed at William Morris by ensuring there was another job for me there. That way, he could keep his eye on me every day. He knew where I was, and what I was doing. I wasn't leaving. And he knew I was nearby if he needed my experienced help. I turned the tables—it was now George who wanted that loyal and respected friend around.

Lee Karsian was an agent in the TV commercial department at William Morris. Without my knowing exactly how it happened, I found myself working for Lee (though now, I'm quite sure George had something to do with it). Back then, though, all I knew was that there was an opening and I took it.

Lee was married to the comedian Pat Carroll. He was a difficult guy, terribly insecure, and after a while he complained to George that I was too aggressive and trying to take over the department. Lee told me, "You know what George Wood said when I told him about you? He said, 'Fuck him. Fire him.'"

"Then why don't you?" I asked.

"Because I'm a good guy," said Lee.

What George *really* told Lee was, "It's not in your best interest to fire him." That's how George operated. He wanted me near. I mean, say you're Lee Karsian and you've got George Wood's guy—the guy who's worked with him for over two years. He knows things. Are you going to fire him? No. Lee changed the story to make himself look good.

The truth is, I wasn't trying to take over the department. I realized the only way I could move up the ladder was to expand our TV commercial department by signing up top models; I signed legendary American model Suzy Parker and actress-model Diahn Williams, both of whom became frequent guests on *The Tonight Show*.

Lee hated my street smarts. But the way things worked, we all tried to book clients within the department, regardless of the agent.

One time I was in my office talking to Suzy Parker. I was just about to give her some good news—that I'd set her up with a national commercial that came with huge residuals—when Lee walked in.

"Take a letter, kiddo," he said. It was an attempt to humiliate me in front of my client.

Rather than punch him in the neck, I said, "You should learn dictation."

He shrugged and turned toward the door. As he walked out, he asked, "Did you buy that suit new?"

He didn't know the suit was one of Mr. Lastfogel's hand-me-downs, though he may have been able to tell that it had cost more than his entire wardrobe. I didn't say anything. But the snarkiness, which I'd always been able to handle by staying above it, was wearing thin.

I didn't like Lee at all. He was nasty and treated me deplorably. I may have taken it from George Wood, but I wouldn't take it from Karsian—I mean, who the hell was he? Was I being aggressive? Sure. But I was making commissions. Lee wasn't. Now, Lee *could* have fired me if he'd wanted to badly enough. He could have marched into the personnel department and said, "He's not doing his job. He's got to go." And that would have been that. Instead, he went to George. The truth is, Lee was afraid of George, and when George said, "You can't fire him," Lee backed down. Not long after that I was promoted, and I was finally on my way.

* * *

I was always moving further away from the Red Mill, but I never forgot it.

One time when I was a kid, I was getting a haircut with my father. My dad had been a very handsome man, but he'd let himself fall apart. He was broken down, his teeth were bad, and his life was going nowhere. The barber, who took care of a lot of the guys at the Red Mill, said, "Schwartzy, how'd you get such a nice kid?" That upset both my dad and me. I looked straight ahead and said nothing. It was demeaning, and while my father was proud of me, that crack hurt. I suppose I took in those kinds of comments and decided that maybe I could be the man that Schwartzy wasn't. My father was called "Schwartzy," but I wanted to be "Mr. Schwartz." And so that's who I became. I was Mr. Schwartz from then on.

* * *

I met Merv Griffin at *The Tonight Show*. I'd gotten my promotion and was no longer George's assistant, but I wasn't quite sure where to go next. I was thinking about doing nightclubs, but George suggested the TV department to me. He said, "You don't want to be in the nightclub business; it's not for you." It was like Moe Gold was speaking to me all over again, an echo from the Red Mill reverberating across the years.

"I hate TV," I said. All I was interested in were the Copa Girls, the dancers brought to fame by Barry Manilow's song "Copacabana (At the Copa)." But George was right, and I was assigned to book William Morris acts on *The Tonight Show*. Johnny Carson was set to host *The Tonight Show* on NBC, beginning in the fall. However, he was contracted to host a game show, *Who Do You Trust?*, on ABC until then.

Because NBC was waiting for Johnny Carson's contract to run out at ABC before Carson could take over *The Tonight Show* from Jack Paar, I was tasked with booking guest hosts for a week at a time throughout the summer. I booked the comedian Jack Carter, as well as Totie Fields, a very funny lady who'd gotten her big break on *The Ed Sullivan Show* after Ed saw her at the Copacabana.

By the time we met, Merv had been around: He'd been a host on many game shows. He'd hosted *Play Your Hunch* and *Keep Talking* and had guest stints as the host of *The Price Is Right* and *To Tell the Truth*. He'd also been in movies and starred as Woody in *Finian's Rainbow* on Broadway. I could tell he was talented and bright, but it wasn't like I felt he had the eye of the tiger right off the bat or anything—not the way I did with Barbra Streisand.

Merv was struggling to find guests for *The Tonight Show* for the week. His own agency, MCA, wasn't doing the job for him, so I stepped in. "Hey," I said, "I'm with the Morris office. I'd be happy to help you." He accepted my offer, and the rest is history.

I told Merv I knew Suzy Parker, at one time the most famous model in America, and had dated her once or twice. (She was a head taller than me.) With Merv's approval, I booked her for Monday's show. We did a day in the life of a model. I also booked performers from the Second City in Chicago for that week. The guests must have gone over well, because of all those guest hosts that came before Carson, Merv had the highest ratings.

But there was something else that set him apart too: a likability factor. Merv was unassuming and modest. A nice, well-dressed guy with a big laugh. He was good-looking too; he reminded me of Spencer Tracy as a young man. And part of the reason why he was so likable was that he really did like people. He appeared to be in awe of every guest he interviewed. It was sincere too—he *was* in awe. Above all, Merv was genuine; what you saw was what you got. All of that combined with a kind of boyish charm to create a character you couldn't help but want to spend your evenings with.

While Totie Fields and Jack Carter were great fill-ins, I'm not sure they were ever destined to be permanent hosts. They came off a little too aggressive—a little too borscht belt, if I'm being honest. Meanwhile, Merv appealed to the whole country, just like Carson.

Merv also had a great eye for talent. On one episode of *The Tonight Show*, singer Tiny Tim married Victoria Budinger (better known as "Miss Vicki" at the time) in front of forty million people. It's still the highest-rated late-night show episode ever. It was Merv who found Tiny Tim in the first place. He'd been hanging out in the alleyway next to the Little Theatre, where *The Merv Griffin Show* was filmed, just outside an office doorway. Merv saw him there and instructed a booker to get him on the show.

Merv was willing to gamble. We all were, to some extent; it wasn't just celebrities we'd put on television back then, although sometimes, those unknowns would turn out to be big later on. Woody Allen did stand-up on *The Tonight Show* before anyone knew who he was, and Richard Pryor had his first TV appearance there—all when Merv was hosting.

After I helped him book the show, I could tell Merv was impressed. I also knew his agency, MCA, was going through some government breakups. The Sherman Antitrust Act dictated that MCA couldn't be both an agency representing clients and a production company; it had to choose. While William Morris foolishly chose to remain an agency, MCA's leadership determined it would be better off as a production outfit. The company would eventually take over Universal Pictures, a big win. At the time, though, that decision meant that Merv couldn't stay with MCA.

I'd seen how George would bring clients in. He would begin the relationship and then leave it to somebody else to actually do the business, so that's what I did. I said, "Why don't you come in for a meeting at William Morris?" Except in this case, the guys doing business were a lot more senior than I was. The younger agents were called "The Foot Soldiers," and that was our role: to feed business to the bigger fish.

I'm still impressed with what Merv did the day he came in. There was a big meeting for his signing, and I was at the back of this room with all the younger guys. All the executives were up front, of course. By then, Nat Lefkowitz had taken over as president of William Morris. Nat announced, "Sol Leon will be your prime agent. He's in the TV department."

"Excuse me, gentlemen," said Merv. "I know all of these men by reputation, but I know Murray Schwartz personally, and I know his exuberance, so I want him to be my agent as well."

Mr. Lefkowitz glanced over at me. "Murray, come up front!" he said. George winked at me and mouthed, "Good job, kid." George took great pride in the fact that I'd brought Merv to the Morris office. It was George who'd developed me, and he got a boost out of my success. He was sure to tell everyone that he'd taught me everything I knew. In truth, though, George had taught me more about gambling, schmoozing, drinking, dressing up at night, and how to light a lady's cigarette and stand when she left the table than

101

he'd ever taught me about being a theatrical agent; that I'd learned on my own. But he gave me my break, and I'll always be grateful.

Eventually Merv became a major client, and Sol and I became his co-agents. To this day, I believe the William Morris Agency still receives commissions on *Wheel of Fortune* and *Jeopardy!* from the package deals I made back then when I was his agent—that is, if Sony hasn't by this time renegotiated the deal.

But things weren't going nearly as well for me at home as they were professionally. Merv had a wife, Julann, and a son, Tony. They lived in a lovely apartment on Central Park West. By all accounts, they had a wonderful home life. Since I was moving up the ladder, Ann and I had moved to an apartment on the east side of Manhattan. We must've looked like we were doing pretty well ourselves. But by this time, things weren't going well with Ann. Maybe it was a lack of maturity or judgment—a decision that was a product of the times, when people married at a much younger age. Looking back, I think it would've been better for me to have met somebody at the Red Mill, to marry a woman from the place I'd come from—though in those days, the dancers weren't the kind of girls you'd marry.

But I didn't marry a girl from the Red Mill. I married Ann, and she had a nervous breakdown.

I can't blame Ann. Her father was an alcoholic, and she grew up in a brutal environment. One night before we were married, I was walking her home after a date—we'd gone to see a movie and have an ice cream soda—and we found Ann's father lying in the street, drunk, his head resting on the curb. She started to walk by. "That's your father," I said. "We can't leave him."

"Leave him," she said.

I didn't leave him. Instead, I called a cab and helped him get home. Ann walked away. I didn't understand at the time. I thought it was so sad for her, but I didn't really grasp how much of an impact experiences like that had had on her throughout her life.

We eloped shortly after I returned from the service. Our siblings served as witnesses, and right after, we took off for our honeymoon in Bermuda. We stayed at the Princess Hotel. The same set of songs piped through the hotel's music system. Over and over again, I would hear Bette Midler singing "Everything's Coming Up Roses":

You'll be swell,

You'll be great,

Gonna have the whole world on the plate.

I was sure she was right. Ann and I were newly married and in love. After the honeymoon, we moved to Forest Hills, an upper-middle-class neighborhood in Queens. I was making good money, and soon we were able to buy a beach cottage in Amagansett, which would eventually become chic and expensive. All of our friends were getting married too. It was the thing to do back then—get married young, start a family. And I was ready to be a family man. Our life together felt new and different, sophisticated. We went to Broadway shows and out to dinner in the city. It felt as if we were on track toward a brilliant future together, one I'd only recently begun to understand.

But all wasn't as well as it seemed. Ann's illness revealed itself slowly, but I wasn't really looking at first. She was obsessed with cleanliness, bringing Lysol and her own pillowcases wherever we went. At first I saw this as an adorable quirk. But things we think are cute when we're young are one day revealed to be terribly neurotic. Eventually I realized that these tendencies were just plain crazy. Over time, Ann became obsessive-compulsive. Things were going badly, and I saw that I'd made a big mistake. Ann had serious problems, far more serious than I could have recognized when we first said "I do." She was diagnosed with paranoid schizophrenia.

As Ann's condition worsened, I had her transferred from the Payne Whitney Psychiatric Clinic to Gracie Square Hospital, both on the Upper East Side of Manhattan. It was the best facility I knew of, and I couldn't really afford it, but it was my best hope for Ann. Her parents and brother refused to help—they wouldn't give me a nickel—so I was stuck with enormous hospital bills. I was broke and having a horrible time.

Meanwhile, Ann was undergoing shock therapy at the hospital, and that didn't sit well with me. Just looking at her, you could see she was stunned. Her doctors were also giving her Thorazine, a powerful antipsychotic drug. *What do I know? I'm not a doctor*, I thought. Those were the tools they had to treat schizophrenia at the time. But I could see how out of it she was. Do we treat schizophrenia any better now? Judging from the number of homeless people on the streets of Los Angeles, I'd argue that we still have a ways to go.

Even though I was uncomfortable with the effects of Ann's treatment, I took our daughter Suzy to see her on Thanksgiving. Suzy was seven years old at the time and she'd been looking forward to this moment for weeks. As we waited for Ann to come downstairs to the visitor's room, I could feel Suzy's excitement. She pulled away from me and ran to the hallway to wait for her mother in front of the elevator, shortening the distance between them as much as possible.

The elevator doors opened, and there stood Ann, looking sullen and very thin. She stepped over the threshold and stared at us for a brief moment, her face blank. Then she turned around and walked back into the elevator, the doors shutting behind her. Her rejection of us both was mute and final. I remember saying, "Oh my God." *What had she done to her own child?*

I was completely overwhelmed. By then, we'd had another baby, Jennifer, and I was struggling to care for both kids and keep my head above water at work. Early on, I'd decided that I wanted to learn from George without becoming him—but I was so unhappy that I very nearly did become George. My world was falling apart, and it was starting to show at work. I was no longer that fair-haired boy; I couldn't concentrate. My star was no longer on the rise at William Morris. In fact, it felt like my star was dropping from the sky. I missed hours every day just trying to handle my personal life.

I knew I needed help. But it wasn't going to come from my family, and I was embarrassed to talk to my friends about it. We didn't speak of mental illness in those days. Analysis was frowned upon too—those who needed it were considered nuts. But I was facing an impossible situation, balancing a fractured home life with the demands of my expanding career, and getting professional help was my only hope.

I started to interview therapists. I'd already met two I didn't like. One guy was bald, with a head that shined as brightly as the big clock in his office. That clock ticked loudly, counting down every expensive minute of my appointment. He sat behind a desk and I sat in front of it. I'd always pictured lying on a small leather couch, a shrink perched just behind my right shoulder, the way Freud did it. (Though later on I read Freud only did that because he just couldn't look at people anymore—there wasn't some profound reason behind it. In some cases, a cigar is just a cigar, and a seat is just a seat.)

I was feeling pretty defeated when a friend said, "Go see Margaret Wreschner." Like many Manhattan therapists at the time, Miss Wreschner lived and worked in a handsome brownstone on Riverside Drive.

The day of my first appointment, I walked all the way from Sixth Avenue to Riverside, right across Central Park, probably as a form of avoidance, a way of delaying the encounter. It was a hot summer afternoon, and I remember I was wearing an uncomfortable suit, completely wrong for walking that far in the heat. I was sweating and everything was sticking to me. I thought, "I'd better like this woman."

After walking halfway across New York City and through the park, I climbed up four flights of stairs to get to her office, and I was tired. At the time I was smoking a lot of cigarettes, and I was pretty close to burnout. Actually, I'd passed burnout several exits back and was barreling toward a nervous breakdown of my own. I threw my jacket on the couch and said, "Could you turn on the fuckin' air conditioning?"

"Yes, of course," she said in German-accented English. "All you have to do is ask. It's your hour." I liked her immediately.

And so, Miss Wreschner became my therapist. When I got to her, I was a mess. My life was crumbling. Ann's mental illness had progressed to the point where she'd already been committed. Nothing was working anymore. I was in trouble, and I knew it. "What do I do?" I asked her.

Miss Wreschner was blunt. "Three people can survive," she said, "or all four of you are going to drown."

Miss Wreschner wasn't like other therapists, who dig deep into your childhood to get to the root of your issues. She was more concerned with my present-day problems than how my mom and dad had treated me. And rather than just listen quietly and make me decide for myself, a common therapeutic practice, she talked a lot. Occasionally I'd ask her questions about herself too. One time she told me she was leaving for a trip to Europe. "Who are you going with?" I asked.

"Well," she said, "I usually don't discuss that."

"C'mon," I said.

"I'm going alone," she told me.

"Do you get lonely?" I asked.

"Sometimes I do, sometimes I don't." She didn't share a lot about herself, but for a guy who was pretty lonely himself—desperate for human connection and comfort—it was just enough. She was so empathetic and insightful.

Later on, I learned she was a Holocaust survivor, making it through three different camps before she was able to come to America. I didn't know it at the time—she never mentioned it—but I'm sure what she'd been through had a lot to do with how she treated me. And that treatment had a profound impact on my life.

As much as I liked her, and as much as I thought therapy was working for me, I reached a point where I felt I couldn't afford it anymore. Sessions were costly back then, just as they are today, and the bills for Ann's care were piling up. When I brought up that concern at my next appointment, Miss Wreschner asked in her German accent, "How much do you smoke a week?"

I told her, and she took out a piece of paper and a pen. She was quiet for a moment as she jotted something down. Then she handed the paper to me. "This is what you pay for your cigarettes every month," she said. "Stop smoking. This is better for you."

* * *

I suppose my early life was damaging. Many people's lives are. I had to resolve my issues. The life I'd pursued, the life I'd run from the Red Mill to find, was utterly unlike the life in which I now found myself. And I'd have to change it yet again for my own sake, and that of my kids.

Ann's appeal lay in her glamour. As I've said, my pursuit of glamour led me to this big stage on which my life has played out—but in the case of my marriage, my yearning for it took me down a dark path. George's weakness got him into gambling; mine brought me to Ann. With time, I've been able to see that the attraction to a particular look can be as inborn as any other personality trait. How are we to predict where our tendencies will bring us?

Ann kept a scrapbook of everything I'd given her, and the book was filled with love letters and notes, playbills, records of everything we did. She'd kept mementos of all those things. There were the programs and ticket stubs from *My Fair Lady*, references to books we'd read, and dried flowers. It was the sweetest thing that had ever been done for me. When she was in the mental hospital, I wrote in the scrapbook, "To my unique rose," a line taken from *The Little Prince*. I did love her, and for her, I became a romantic young man.

The people in our lives bring out qualities we can't see in ourselves, and no matter how things turn out, it's through relationships that we discover a great deal about who we are. I had no idea how much I was about to learn.

CHAPTER 10

"Bring the Baby"

After all the time I'd spent with George, the effort of building a career, and handling my difficult marriage, I wasn't functioning well anymore. It had all become overwhelming, and the fun was gone. Besides that, Sol, Merv's other agent, tried to take credit for everything I did. But I had to keep moving forward. What else was I going to do? I needed a paycheck, and Merv needed an agent.

Merv's stint hosting *The Tonight Show* had been so successful that NBC gave him his own daytime talk show. Merv had a natural gift for the talk show format. It was met with critical acclaim. Intellectuals loved it; college students did too. But the ratings were garbage. Having worked in television long enough, I knew it wasn't too smart for TV—it was too smart for *daytime* TV. It just didn't do well. Barely a year in, it was canceled. The fans who loved it wrote letters—tens of thousands of them—protesting the cancellation, but it didn't do any good.

When his show got canceled on NBC, Merv didn't know what to do. His movie career wasn't going anywhere. Theater just provided an occasional job here and there. He wasn't a singer's singer—he'd done "I've Got a Lovely Bunch of Coconuts," a novelty song that certainly wasn't going to get him any record contracts. Merv thought he might leave the business. Maybe he'd work for an ad agency.

I didn't know what to do either. The Morris office had thought, *This guy is going to be big*, and they had me dedicating virtually all of my time to Merv. If he left to join an ad agency, I didn't have a big client. I'd get 10 percent of nothing.

I began searching for other options for Merv. I called summer stock theaters to see if they had any roles for him. I even went to the library to see if there were plays he could be in. We were desperate.

There was one offer on the table, though. Westinghouse had offered Merv the chance to host his own show on Channel 11, a local channel—it would just air in New York City. The powers at William Morris didn't like that. "You don't want your career to end up being one local station in New York," they told him. But what other option did he have?

One day we took a cab ride through Central Park. Merv was still mulling over what to do. "What are your thoughts?" he asked me.

"Merv," I said, "TV is important. It's the future. Even though all of the powers that be think the Westinghouse gig will be the end of your career, I think you should take it. Who knows? It could lead to other shows on other stations." I have to admit, it was selfish. If he were to leave, I'd have to find another client, and I'd been completely focused on him. But he'd have to build a career from scratch too.

Merv thought about it, then nodded. "OK, let's do it." So we made the deal.

The summer before the show began, Merv was in two summer stock plays, *The Tender Trap*, and *Come Blow Your Horn* with William

Bendix. He broke all kinds of records. Everyone loved him. I would travel with him and be there to read notes.

That fall, *The Merv Griffin Show* began filming at the Little Theatre in New York, which is now called the Helen Hayes Theater. Merv liked an intimate theater where he could be close to the audience, and the Little Theatre was great for that. It was also next to the celebrity haunt Sardi's, making it the perfect place to drum up talent. Sometimes we would just head next door, pull people out of Sardi's, and bring them over to do the show. That practice gave the show a natural, free-spirited vibe—it was great show business.

Merv's show took off, and we began booking more and more stations—another 155, to be exact. It became big time.

Merv also decided to bring on Arthur Treacher as his sidekick. Treacher had made a career playing the butler in a number of films, including four of Shirley Temple's movies. He was a big guy, six foot four, and he liked to drink. He almost fell down the stairs at Sardi's a few times, he was so drunk. In fact, one night before the show, he fell asleep in the Sardi's phone booth. He would snooze on the show too—just doze off in the middle of things—and someone would have to poke him to wake him up. But he was a great guy—just the sweetest. He called Merv "Mervin," and I called him "Mr. Treacher."

One night they were filming *The Merv Griffin Show* in Vegas. Lee Solomon, a nightclub agent at William Morris, had been the one to book the show. Since Merv was my client, though, I was there to take care of him and his interests. Lee was a character. He wore big, bold cufflinks. He called everyone "cookie" and "lamb chop" and "sweetheart." I've never had anyone call me "lamb chop" in my life—except for Lee. Lee came backstage, looked at Arthur, and said, "Hey, Artie baby."

Treacher stood up. "Never call me Artie, you putz," he said. It was hilarious. He was wonderful, and Merv's decision to get a sidekick like Arthur Treacher was a testament to his own great instincts.

* * *

Merv did so well at Westinghouse that we got approached by CBS. They wanted him to go opposite Carson, an offer that was very tempting to Merv. So we made the deal, and he got the Cort Theatre on 48th Street. Hedy Lamarr was one of the guests on the premiere—not bad for your first show. But after a while, ratings were terrible.

Merv decided to move to California. In New York, he wasn't only airing directly opposite Carson—he was competing with him for guests. California, he figured, would open up a whole new world of guests. He was spot-on with his decision. With the show in California, he wasn't going toe-to-toe with Carson for talent. Still, the plethora of guests didn't do much to improve ratings.

With ratings tanking, things weren't looking good at CBS, so we approached Al Krivin, the president of Metromedia, and asked if he'd bring us back. He agreed, telling us he'd syndicate the show. That meant we could sell it to local stations rather than just a single national network. With syndication, there would be more opportunity and more cash to go around. But there was a catch: if we left CBS voluntarily, there was a substantial financial penalty. However, if CBS was the one to sever ties, it would have to pay us. Fortunately, it decided not to renew us, and we were free to go.

At that point, I had such latitude on the *The Merv Griffin Show*, I could book anyone I wanted. Merv would ask who was available, and if we had a big star in town—Jack Lemmon, for instance—I could say, "Hey, Merv, I got Jack Lemmon, but I need two singers, or two comics." I was leveraging. And that was fine with Merv.

In my personal life, though, I was still feeling pretty helpless.

Ann was eventually released from the hospital and allowed to come home. By that point we had two children—Suzy, our oldest, and her baby sister, Jenny. My mother helped watch the kids while I worked all day. It was the one time my mother jumped in to help me, but I was still responsible for keeping house.

Meanwhile, Ann wouldn't put Jenny down. I'd bought a new crib and stroller, but she didn't want to use them. Instead, she would carry Jenny constantly, walking around the neighborhood for hours while one of our mothers—Ann's or mine—stayed with Suzy.

And then one night she didn't come home. No one knew where she was.

We had a little beach cottage at the time. I'd closed the house for the season, since it was starting to get cold and it didn't have any heat, but my neighbors at that place called and reported they'd seen Ann at the house. They'd also given Jenny some milk and food. "Ann looks awful," they told me; they said she looked decrepit, weak, and tragic. Then they told me they'd seen her getting on a train; she wasn't there anymore. Later I'd learn that she had gone to stay with her brother in New Jersey, but it would take a long time to figure that out.

Meanwhile, Merv had presented me with an opportunity. He said, "How about you come out to California and help me build a company?" I came to the conclusion that I had nothing to lose.

Though I wasn't quite sure of my decision, I told Miss Wreschner I was leaving New York and wouldn't be seeing her again. Then I asked her, as a farewell gesture, if she would go to dinner with me. She said that never, ever would she have dinner with a client. "In your case, though, because you're leaving, I will," she said.

We went to dinner at a Spanish restaurant in the same building as the William Morris offices—1350 Avenue of the Americas. We talked a long time, and she said, "Usually I tell people that when they leave their surroundings, they don't understand that their head travels with them. I say that attempting to leave your problems behind is not a healthy way to go through life. But I believe you're a different story. It's time to move on from your wife."

I called Merv two days later and said, "I'll quit William Morris if you still want me to build a company."

"When are you coming out?" he replied. It was decided: I would sell my profit sharing at William Morris to pay for Ann's hospital bills and, "Go West, young man."

It was a good business decision, but it was an even better life decision. It was a decision for my own survival.

Going out to meet Merv in California was a gamble, though—and one I don't think I'd ever have taken again. I had no money, I didn't have a partner, and I had two small children I was going to have to raise on my own while undertaking this enormous task on the other side of the country—and one of those children was still missing, along with her mother.

It was Miss Wreschner who encouraged me. What if she hadn't? What if I'd stayed at William Morris? I think I would have been fired—and soon. Thankfully, I made different arrangements.

The next step was to figure out the logistics. No one at the agency could know that I was thinking of leaving before I had all the puzzle pieces in place. I flew out to Los Angeles in secret, for a single day, to look for a house. I got a map, located the school I wanted Suzy and Jenny to attend, and drew a circle around it. My home would have to sit somewhere inside that circle. The house we first lived in was rented after a two-minute look inside. "It'll do just fine," I said, and then I got on a plane back to New York.

With all of that settled, I headed to the William Morris offices and told Sol I was resigning. He asked where I was going.

"I'm starting a company with Merv Griffin."

"That's what I should have done," said Sol. But I knew he never would have taken the chance.

The day I moved to Los Angeles, I had $400 in cash in my pocket and one daughter with me, Suzy, who was seven years old. Jenny was still missing. I got Suzy settled in LA with a wonderful nanny, Mrs. Murphy (who had a charming Irish brogue), and a housekeeper named Shirley, a black lady with the biggest smile I'd ever seen and the best recipe for New Orleans gumbo I'd ever tasted.

Then I came back to New York to search for Jenny. The contacts I'd made through George came in handy in ways I couldn't have imagined, and it was his "friends" who found Jenny for me. She was with her mother in a seedy hotel on 48th Street. Child services took Jenny at first, and then Ann's brother cared for her while I tended to the legal arrangements—I had to get custody of my daughter, which meant I had to fight for her in court.

Why didn't the judge grant it to me automatically? I don't really know the answer. Perhaps it was because I'd taken Suzy to California—and out of the jurisdiction of New York—without anyone's permission. Maybe it was because the judge saw me as this big, fancy executive who thought he didn't have to abide by the rules. Or maybe it was because back then, it was incredibly unusual for a man to have sole custody of his children. Whatever her reason, she certainly wasn't interested in cutting me any slack.

A new court date was set every week. For weeks I flew back and forth from Los Angeles to New York to appear in court to try to gain custody. I'd take a red-eye the night before a court appearance because I had to be there at nine in the morning. Ann would never show up. Then I'd get back on the plane at 3 p.m. New York time to be in the studio in LA by eight. After a couple of months of this, I was worn thin by the pressure of the new job and all the back-and-forth. In my anxiety over the failure to resolve Jenny's status, I blew up at the judge.

"You can't keep asking me to come here every Wednesday. I have to fly back the same day!"

She pushed back, and I got nastier. "I will hold you in contempt of court," she said, threatening me.

I told her, "Go fuck yourself. Go ahead, why don't you lock me up now? You'll be on national television tonight on *The Merv Griffin Show*. I'll be in contempt? Why don't you fuckin' lock me up right now?" In truth, I think I was looking to get locked up to get some attention for the case.

"We're done here," she said, shaking her head, and the hearing was over. But there still had been no decision. I think I flew to New York four or five times, but it felt like a hundred, without any movement on the custody question.

After my blowup, the case was reassigned to another judge and I got a new court date. So I returned to New York again. Jenny was with her uncle, monitored by child services. Ann still hadn't shown up to any of the court appearances, and she didn't show up this time either.

The new judge asked me how many times I'd traveled to New York for the case. Then he asked if Jenny's mother was in attendance. I said no, and he said, "Award this man custody of both children. This case is over."

116

Then he asked me to come with him to his chambers. He was a distinguished-looking black man with gray hair, just like a judge out of a movie. In fact, *everything* was beginning to feel like it was happening in a movie. How could all of this be real? Ann never showed up. I had to beg for my child. The hours logged on jets blurred one into the other. Sometimes I wasn't sure in which direction I was flying.

Jenny was never on any of the flights. She was never there, and Ann was never there. It was just me, standing powerless before these judges, caught in a dreadful stalemate. Jenny was getting older as the talks dragged on, and I know I felt much, much older as the weeks stacked up. I'd been the favorite at William Morris, "the kid," rising through the ranks, sharply dressed and scoring new business without appearing to break a sweat. Now here I was, about to be a single father, starting all over again in a new state, with new people and responsibilities, and all I wanted was to take my baby with me and to give her a real home. I was a long way from the magical spell of the Red Mill, and my early days with George were fading from view.

Sometimes, on the flight back to California, I'd light a cigarette and have a drink, look out at the blue sky in which I seemed to be permanently suspended, and think about working as a stagehand at the Red Mill. "Turn the lights to blue, Sonny," I'd hear a voice in my head say, and I'd remember the comfort of the blue glow. The patrons looked comforted too, as the blue shadows erased the lines from their careworn faces. Whatever followed you up to the door of the Red Mill was left outside for a while.

The day the case was settled and I was finally awarded custody of Jenny, the judge had only two things he wanted to say to me in the privacy of his chambers: "If you ever open your mouth again to a judge in my court, I *will* lock you up. Now get out of here and have a good life."

That day I took Jennifer.

She wasn't even two yet, and I had nothing for a baby. I bought a plastic TWA shoulder bag, a couple of diapers and T-shirts, and got on the plane. We flew first class. Here I was, carrying this baby on my lap with nothing a child might want on a trip. There was no special food for her, so I gave her a lamb chop, the same thing George had once offered me when I was sick.

It was a strange, surprising, miraculous day. This time, when I looked out at the sky, it seemed we were moving through it at the speed of sound. And when I thought of the Red Mill, I heard Joe Duro and his trumpet on the Fourth of July, the house decorated for the occasion with red, white, and blue flowers on every table: "*Off we go, into the wild blue yonder . . .*"

Off we go, indeed.

* * *

To this day, I have no idea what became of Ann. She never even tried to see Suzy and Jenny. Eventually, even though it had been years since I'd heard from her, I still had to go through the formalities of a divorce. I hired an attorney and we went to court. My attorney also happened to be the mayor of Beverly Hills at the time, which added yet another surreal detail to the proceedings. The judge asked me, "Is your wife here?"

"No."

"Can you define your irreconcilable differences?"

"She disappeared five years ago and I haven't seen or heard from her since."

"There are children?"

"Yes, and they've never heard from her."

"I'd say that's irreconcilable. I suggest that we grant this man's divorce, but it must be done formally." So, as a formality, an ad was placed in the newspaper: I publicized that I was divorcing, and I was divorced. Finally, it was done.

* * *

Perhaps because of her earliest experiences, Jenny seemed to be able to handle changing situations. One time our nanny, Mrs. Murphy, got sick on the day that I had a major meeting with John Kluge, the CEO and owner of Metromedia. I called all over town trying to find a replacement babysitter for the day but couldn't find anyone who could help. I called Merv in a panic. Merv said, "Bring the baby."

"Bring a baby to negotiate a multimillion-dollar deal?"

"Yeah. I'll help with her. It'll be OK." And so, over wedge salads and steaks at the historic Hollywood Boulevard restaurant Musso & Frank—the showbiz haunt made famous by the show *The Kominsky Method* on Netflix and the film "Once Upon a Time in Hollywood"—the three of us took turns holding Jenny on our laps. It was a great meeting, and we made a deal worth millions to extend Merv's contract in prime time.

Merv was always generous with his time when it came to the kids. I was a bachelor father, but Merv was always right there, ready to help make it work, no matter what. There were times when I had to run out of a meeting to take care of my children, and he was always kind and respectful. He understood. As a result, I was very loyal to him, and I protected him. Recalling these events, which were so sweet, makes the reality of the present situation all the more painful.

We became like family, and we had some very happy times. One year my housekeeper, Shirley, cooked a goose on Christmas Day. I invited Susan Stafford, whom I was dating at the time; Susan was the original co-host of *Wheel of Fortune*, before Vanna White.

I'd hired waiters for the occasion, and we were having a great time. Shirley had had a little to drink while she cooked, and when she brought out the goose, it slipped off the tray and fell onto the floor. Without missing a beat, she went back into the kitchen and returned with another goose, beautifully dressed and ready to be served, and as she set it on the table, she said, "Good I made two, huh?"

For the Thanksgivings that followed, I would take my kids up to visit Merv in Carmel, where his mother and sisters lived, and we'd all have dinner together at Pebble Beach. That gave Suzy, Jenny, and me a sense of family that was lacking in our lives. Merv and I knew each other's problems. He was close to my kids, and I was close to his son, Tony—so much so that when it was time for Tony to be confirmed in the Catholic Church and choose a middle name, he asked if he could be called Murray Schwartz.

Things never quite worked out with my actual family. My parents and the people back in the Bronx never knew about my success. My father died young, just as I was getting ready to marry Ann. My mother was detached, aloof, an ephemeral kind of person, drifting in and out of the frame. She simply didn't seem to want to know what I was doing. That faraway look in her eyes—the look she'd had when she sipped her manhattans at the bar of the Red Mill—had become fixed.

After my father died, there was no longer any reason for me to go to the Bronx. The Red Mill was over for me. The neighborhood had changed, and everyone I knew there had either died or moved away. Years later Anja, a woman I was seeing at the time, said, "Let's go up to the Bronx. I want to see where you came from. I want to see the Red Mill."

"We can't go there now," I said. "It's a war zone."

"I'm going whether you go or not," said Anja.

I was right. It was a war zone. The Bronx had changed so much I didn't recognize it. But then again, so had I.

My dad, Irv, holding a shillelagh at the Red Mill bar.

The sleeve that
photographs
were placed in
after a couple got
their photograph
taken.

A typical pair
of couples on a
night out at the
Red Mill.

*George and Lois O'Brien,
his soon-to-be-wife. One of the few
photos of George out there.*

*Jimmy Blue Eyes Alo. He was often
referred to as the "gentleman's gangster."*

Me being interviewed by Merv after my return from Uganda.

*Sammy Davis Jr. and me when he was
a guest on our show, Dance Fever.*

When I got back from Uganda,
the LA Times did a front page story on my return.

Merv, Prime Minister Rabin of the State of Israel,
Mrs. Rabin, and me, needing a haircut.

Prince Rainier, Princess Grace, me, Princess Antionette (whose daughter, Christina, and I became dear friends), and Merv.

Bob Murphy, Merv, and me at the after party, celebrating Merv's last show (he was on air for twenty-five years).

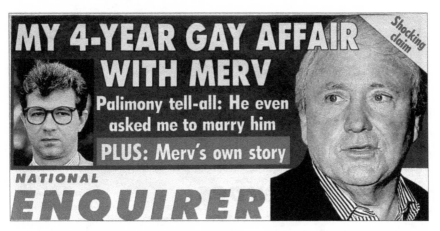

The National Enquirer article that came out about Merv.

CHAPTER 11

"Did He Just Buy It?"

Merv and I had some really big wins together. We came up with ideas that changed not only our careers, but show business itself. And sometimes the best ideas arrived in the most uneventful ways. I'd just spent a rainy weekend in Califon, New Jersey, where Merv had a little farm. We were driving back to the city in a limousine—Merv; his wife, Julann; his son, Tony; game show producer Ron Greenberg; and me.

Julann had always been kind of kooky and fun. "Gee," she said, "I got an idea. Why don't we play a game where I give you the answer and you give me the question?" That idea set off sparks in Merv, and it would ultimately have a tremendous impact on our careers: it would become one of the longest-running game shows in television history—*Jeopardy!*

We played that game all the way home, and shortly after we got back to the city, Merv got a group of people together and began developing it for TV.

Creating a game show is all about trial and error, and rather than invest a lot of dough in it up front, we wanted to hammer out the details first. Thus, the early stages always seemed a little unsophisticated. They happened in an office, rather than on a set. Everyone would gather around a table and pitch different ideas: *Does this work? How about that? Throw in a gimmick, like Double Jeopardy.*

One element to grapple with was the challenge of coming up with the questions. Ron Greenberg suggested making the questions difficult. Merv was against that, but Ron was right on target: the difficulty of the game, the fact that you've got to be really smart to play, is part of why people still watch *Jeopardy!* today. Viewers admire the ability of the contestants to answer difficult questions on everything from homophones to opera.

But Merv wasn't one to give anyone credit. He had a way of ignoring an idea someone would throw out, only to bring it up as his own idea a few minutes later. Eventually he determined Ron was right about the difficulty of the questions, though he wouldn't say so.

While the questions were tough, the idea behind *Jeopardy!* was extremely simple. It was the same one Julann had come up with during that rainy car ride: *I'll give you the answer and you give me the question.* Ultimately, that simplicity is the key to a good game show. Over the years, people would pitch me their game show ideas—memos or scripts laying out what they'd dreamed up. Anytime a thick stack of paper arrived on my desk, I knew it wouldn't work; the ideas within were just too complex. Those fat envelopes got stamped "unopened and not read" and sent on their way.

On the other hand, with a simple framework in place, you can get into the nitty-gritty, as we did with *Jeopardy!*: *How many categories should there be? How many questions? Should the questions be as difficult as Ron Greenberg wants? What does the show's timing look like?*

All that got hammered out in the conference room. I was still working at William Morris at the time, so I wasn't involved with the actual development of the show, but I knew it was good, and I would always go down to the office conference room where they were working on it and participate as one of the contestants.

The materials we used were rudimentary too. The key piece—that famous *Jeopardy!* board—was created out of cardboard, with little slits in it where the envelopes with the answers would go. It was the precursor to the fancy electronics that would take its place; we needed to avoid incurring any unnecessary expenses.

With the game board built, it was time to bring in real contestants to play the game the way they would on TV—just without the host, the set, and the electronics. The cardboard was the stand-in for all that, with two guys standing behind it and feeding the answers through those slits. Only after we got money to make the pilot would we bring in the stuff you see on the screen.

I'm sure the process is much different today. Big corporations pour big money into efforts like this now, so things probably look much more sophisticated from the get-go. But back then, as a small operation, we weren't about to spend hundreds of thousands of dollars on something that had no guarantee of selling. That simplicity was based on necessity.

When we were confident that the idea was fully developed, we went to NBC's iconic 30 Rockefeller Center to present it to Pat Weaver, who was the network's president at the time. Along with a few young guys who were working for us, we carried the cardboard placard with the envelopes up the street and into the building.

I was there representing William Morris and Merv. This was my big time. As we rode up in the elevator, I thought, *Oh man, this is it. I'm talking to Pat Weaver and selling this game. Who would have thought this would happen?*

Pat was popular and well known. Back then, people in programming were famous—unlike today, when no one knows the executives running the businesses that are omnipresent in our lives. Everything has gotten too corporate now, and there are just too many outlets. But when I was cutting my teeth in the industry, there were just three networks, and these were the guys in charge. They were powerful, and that made them household names.

We had an appointment, and when we arrived at Pat's office, there were all these suits sitting around. I was yet another suit, of course. That was the rule at William Morris: a dark suit and white shirt and tie—and the glamour and sophistication of it all appealed to me.

We started showing Pat our concept for the game—we'd provide the answers and the contestants would provide the questions. We hadn't even finished a round before Pat yelled out, "Buy it!"

With that, he stood up. "Nice to see you guys," he said, and he waved and walked out, leaving his subordinates to take care of the details.

Merv leaned over to me. "Did he just buy it?"

"I don't know," I whispered. "He said 'buy it.'" All we knew was that he hadn't thrown us out.

Moments later we were negotiating the pilot, right there on the spot. It was that quick—no committees, no nothing. Pat had just yelled "Buy it!" and said, "Nice to see you guys" and walked out. That was it.

I was impressed by everything about him. If someone were to play him in a movie today, there would be no better actor for the role than *Mad Men*'s John Slattery. A tall, slim Connecticut guy with gray hair, Pat was as sophisticated as could be. What he was wearing is still imprinted on my mind: gray flannel slacks, black loafers, and red socks. I loved the look of it. To this day, I wear loafers and red socks in the winter, just like he did.

I felt impressive in my own way too. I'd learned to make package deals—on *Jeopardy!*, for example, the deal was not only for Merv but for the entire show. That meant the agency would get 10 percent of the profits from the whole shebang, rather than just 10 percent of an individual's salary. The deal I made was so good, I think William Morris is still pulling a profit from it today.

With Pat's sign-off, we had the opportunity to develop a pilot for the show, to take the idea from cardboard to reality and actually build that *Jeopardy!* wall. What we came up with is pretty much the same as what you see on television today. The electronics got much better, of course, as did the host, and the set is more glamorous. But it's still that same simple idea.

In addition to those difficult questions, *Jeopardy!* would be all about the host. He had to be articulate and able to speak quickly, tossing out answers to obscure questions with ease. Merv always had a good sense of who was a great performer and who wasn't, and he found Art Fleming. Merv had seen Art in an airline commercial and thought he'd be a good fit. Art didn't have any experience hosting, but his agent told him to act like he did during the audition and do his best announcer impression, and that was enough. He nailed it.

Art was a slick guy. He always had a perfect handkerchief in his coat pocket, almost impossibly crisp. We later learned the cloth was wrapped around cardboard. In those days, dry cleaners used to do that, creating little four-point rectangles. Art would just move those handkerchiefs—cardboard and all—from one suit to the next. I thought that was really smart. I actually tried to sell those handkerchiefs, with those perfectly crisp corners (I was always looking for a way to generate dough), but the idea failed.

Art was dignified without being pretentious. His voice had a senatorial quality to it. He was articulate, clear, and beloved by everyone in Nowhere, Middle America. But he was really stiff. He wasn't the kind of guy you'd want to go out and have a drink with. There was no personality to him—he looked as if someone had just wound him up, stuck him in front of the teleprompter, and let him go, reading line for line. Still, Art was the host of *Jeopardy!* for years, and he had a loyal following. It wasn't until the show was revamped for a third time in 1984—twenty years after its debut—that he was replaced.

His successor, Alex Trebek, has been the host ever since. Unlike Art, Trebek has some warmth and style. He's a real personality. And he's smart—being on *Jeopardy!* for thirty-five years, you've got to absorb some of it, right? He's quick and articulate, and he has continued to appeal to new audiences year after year.

* * *

Jeopardy! was created and launched in New York City, and filmed in the same building where we'd pitched it. *Wheel of Fortune*, on the other hand, we developed in California. By then I'd left William Morris and become an integral part of Merv Griffin Enterprises. Merv had absolute and total trust in me. I had the contacts with NBC, and I was the one who would determine whether an idea was salable and how to do it.

Wheel of Fortune is essentially the old kids' game of hangman, where you have to guess the word or phrase in a blank puzzle before you run out of chances. It was Merv's idea to turn it into a game show. As with *Jeopardy!*, the concept is simple, and that's the key to its success.

By then, Merv had also learned from me the concept of OPM— other people's money. We always used NBC's money, not our own, to work out our ideas; we never invested anything up front. I always said, "Let's develop it in the office, and if they're interested, they'll give us a lot of money to make the pilot."

We created *Wheel of Fortune* the same way we'd created *Jeopardy!*—in the office. In place of the cardboard *Jeopardy!* wall, we had a board with letters. We knew we needed a hook, though, and that's where the wheel came into play—a carnival-style game of roulette that could contribute to the excitement.

Creating the wheel itself was a somewhat complex process. The first wheel we developed spun vertically, and we needed to figure out some way to stop it, as well as how to determine what and where the numbers should be. It had to be legitimate, of course, but the odds definitely mattered. I thought, *Where could we get better insight on odds than from my friends in Vegas?* So I flew out there and met with some odds developers at Caesars Palace. Together we came up with a design that would work, adding in a clicker to stop the wheel and figuring out how much each wedge should be worth.

But the show we designed wasn't the *Wheel of Fortune* you know today. When we filmed the pilot in 1973, we called it *Shopper's Bazaar*. Lin Bolen, NBC's vice president of daytime programming, wanted to find a way to appeal to more female viewers. She thought adding a shopping component might be a good idea. Contestants could put the money they earned during each round toward expensive prizes, but they had to solve a word puzzle to win them.

But it wasn't quite simple enough. The rules were complex, and the show itself was boring. Nobody liked the pilot—not Merv, and not Lin.

So we went back to the drawing board to develop a different version, addressing all the aspects of the show that weren't quite right. After we figured it all out, we needed a new name for the show. Late one night in Vegas, it came to me.

I had a couple of bucks to burn, so I went over to gamble at one of the tables. I looked up and there it was: Wheel of Fortune. I called Merv.

"I have the name," I said. "*Wheel of Fortune.*"

"You mean like the song?" he asked. Kay Starr had done a song by that name many years earlier.

"No, no, there's a wheel of fortune here—at the casino."

"Well, let's think about it."

Two days later, he called Lin Bolen and told her that would be the show's name. He just couldn't give credit to anyone else. At the time, it didn't matter to me. I thought, *What the hell's the difference? I'm making good money.* In hindsight that was somewhat foolish, but I didn't know it then.

The first host of *Wheel of Fortune* was Chuck Woolery. Merv saw Chuck playing his guitar someplace and said, "That's our host."

He wanted Susan Stafford, whom I was dating at the time, to turn the letters on the board as Chuck's co-host. I understood why. Susan was gorgeous, one of the most beautiful women I've ever known to this day. She looked just like Bo Derek.

"Merv," I said, "I'm dating her."

"That's fine," he said. "Just don't get into the negotiations." And I didn't.

But in the end, it didn't work out—for *Wheel of Fortune* or my dating life. Oddly enough, both Susan and Chuck would end up answering the Lord's call. That call would take Susan to work with cancer patients in Texas. It would take Chuck elsewhere too, but not quite for the same reasons.

When Susan told me she was going to Texas and why, I was confused. Her work was here, as was her life. I urged her to keep her job, explaining that we'd likely syndicate the show—something I'd learned from our success with *Dance Fever*, a fun disco dance competition we'd created staring Deney Terrio. It was on the air at different times in different cities once a week—mostly on Saturday night. I asked her why she couldn't do the Lord's work and keep her day job. "You could answer the Lord in Los Angeles, on Beverly Boulevard," I said. She told me she couldn't.

One day, shortly after Susan left, Chuck's agent, Dan Stevens, called me.

"Chuck got a message from a higher power," he said.

"Chuck got a message from the Lord?" I asked.

"Yes," his agent replied. "The Lord said it's time to renegotiate his contract." He laughed. Dan knew how ridiculous that sounded, but he felt his hands were tied. "What can I tell you?"

"Unfortunately, I don't have a direct line to Moses—just the William Morris Agency," I told Dan, "and we're not going to renegotiate his contract." I guess Chuck didn't find that funny, because he hated me after that, and he eventually walked, just about seven months after Susan did.

That meant we needed a new host. Merv would always watch TV and call me at home to say he wanted this guy or that one. Pat Sajak was a local Los Angeles weatherman at the time. Merv noticed what a likable guy Pat was—innocuous and Midwestern, with a dry sense of humor. He also noticed an interesting inconsistency. At the beginning of the broadcast, Pat had a small Band-Aid on his left cheek. After the commercial break, Merv noticed that it had migrated to his right cheek. Merv found that hilarious. When he called me to tell me about it, so did I. "He's our guy," Merv said. And he was right again: Pat was a hit with audiences, and today, he's the longest-running game show host on TV. Who would've thought that a single Band-Aid would lead to a thirty-five year career, private planes, the works?

Vanna White took Susan's place as co-host back in 1982. I spotted her backstage when she was on *Dance Fever* as a visiting contestant. My decision to bring her on the show made her life. She has been turning letters ever since.

Eventually *Wheel of Fortune* did go into syndication. After *Dance Fever*'s success, I figured: Why not try to get the rights from NBC to syndicate *Wheel of Fortune* five days a week, in addition to the network show? It seemed like a simple yet smart strategy.

I met Brandon Tartikoff, NBC's young, brilliant head of programming, at Musso & Frank. He was modest, with a serious nature, and he was bringing great ratings to NBC. I suggested that I might make a deal with ABC or CBS at the expiration of our agreement. With that on the table, he initially agreed to grant me the rights—that is, if I would give him a five-year extension on the show. But after a meeting with his legal department, he told me he could only grant me the rights after 6:00 pm, as it might end up going against the network show if it ran on local stations during the day. I was disappointed, but I took the ice-in-winter offer anyway. Plus, getting a five-year extension for a daytime game show was unprecedented back then.

Given the restrictions, though, I was unable to find a syndicator. Metromedia and 20th weren't interested, so I flew to to New York—but things weren't panning out there either. I was staying at the St. Regis and went down to the King Cole Bar, an industry hangout, during cocktail hour. Next to me was a big, loud guy named Bob King. He was talking about syndicating *The Little Rascals*, a kids' show he and his father had owned for many years. It was their lifeblood. I introduced myself and we got to talking. Shortly after, his brother Michael flew in and we made a deal. King World would be our syndicator.

Michael sold the show prime access—the hours between seven and eight in the evening. The ice in winter turned into an oil well. Soon they told us they could sell a one-hour block if we had another show. *Jeopardy!* had been off the air for a handful of years, but I decided to revive it—against Merv's wishes. He didn't want his "baby" in syndication. But Bob Murphy, his childhood buddy and one of Merv Griffin Enterprises' first employees, was able to explain what I was doing, and Merv eventually agreed.

The deal changed the entire structure and value of Merv Griffin Enterprises, and it was one of the primary reasons Coca-Cola bought us years down the line. We had more hours of TV on the air than any other production company. *The Merv Griffin Show* was on for ninety minutes Monday through Friday. *Dance Fever* was on for an hour every Saturday. And *Jeopardy!* and *Wheel of Fortune* were on each day and night. *Headline Chasers*—a game show in which couples faced off with the goal of solving hangman-type puzzles that read like newspaper headlines, then answering questions about the topics revealed—was part of the mix for a year too. That's a lot of hours when you add it up. I guess George Wood was right when he told me to try the TV department.

It paid off for King World too. While our deal stipulated that they couldn't represent any other game shows, they happened to find a young, interesting talk show host in the Midwest—a woman by the name of Oprah Winfrey.

King World eventually went public—something I'd always wanted for Merv Griffin Enterprises. They sold all the company stock to CBS for a cool $2.5 billion. Things didn't go quite that well for Bob King, though. He owned the company with his siblings. Their disagreements drove him to sell out his end for just a few million before King World's big break. His brothers Michael and Roger were really the brains of the operation anyway. Roger had an uncanny memory. His bar bet was to recall the serial numbers on any bill from your pocket. That sure paid off during his travels around the country. Back then, his photographic memory served as the computer for ratings, time periods, and more.

* * *

Once the games got started, they just flowed. Wind up Pat Sajak and he goes out, and Vanna turns around. In fact, Vanna's best interview line ever referenced exactly that. Someone once asked her, "Vanna, how do you keep your job?" "I know the alphabet," she replied. She has a sense of humor about herself and what she does. Both she and Pat perform their roles so seamlessly and have been doing it for so long that people forget there was ever a change of guard. When Pat had to cancel a taping of the show for emergency surgery in November 2019, some news reports stated that he and Vanna had been hosts since the very beginning—that's incorrect, though it certainly feels that way.

I understood the simplicity necessary to create a successful game show, and I loved the challenge of putting those games together, selling them to a network, and getting them on the air. But once they were up and running, they didn't intrigue me anymore. The challenge was over. I had to move on, do something different, keep things interesting. I wasn't content to continue doing the same thing over and over again, the way our hosts were. And that's something I've thought about a lot over the years.

Generating the idea for a successful game show takes a very different kind of intelligence than being a host. Alex, Pat, and Vanna are great at what they do; their longevity certainly speaks to that fact. But despite having tremendous platforms, none of them have ever really been able to harness them to do something more.

Doing what guys like Merv and I did also requires a different kind of brain than you need to be a contestant. I should know: we both took the test to be *Jeopardy!* contestants and failed miserably. If I have any kind of smarts, it's knowing how to take something, leverage it, then sell it to Coca-Cola.

Today there are plenty of people who don't know anything about Merv; they certainly don't have any idea who I am. But they're quite familiar with our success. In all the years that have passed since we developed *Jeopardy!* and *Wheel of Fortune*, there hasn't been another TV game show that has reached the same level. Meanwhile, *Jeopardy!* and *Wheel of Fortune* are still going strong.

CHAPTER 12

The Total Package

After I moved to California, Merv and I got set up. We rented the Hollywood Palace theater on Vine Street. Jerry Lewis's show had been broadcast from that theater, and he and his team had made it beautiful, in a flashy way. They'd upgraded every aspect of it—even the shower had been redone, and the tiles were engraved with his initials. Merv loved it, but the theater wasn't quite intimate enough for him.

At that point, we were handling everything "above the line"—everything you see onscreen: the stars, the guests, the band, the music. Metromedia was taking care of everything below the line, the stuff you don't see: the cameramen, the theater, the props, the sets.

I was ready to shake things up, to take on more . . . and to get Merv the theater he wanted. I took a gamble. If we were responsible for everything—the total package—we could do as we pleased. Plus, I knew that the Celebrity Theater down the block was available, and that the company running it was owned by my old friend Sammy Davis Jr. So I went to Al Krivin at Metromedia and said, "Look, I need more freedom. I want the whole package—above the line and below the line."

Al said, "Murray, that's a big risk. If you take on the whole package and anything goes wrong, it's your problem, not ours. But it's up to you."

Merv asked me if I was sure I could do this. I was.

It was time to do the deal. Sammy's company, which had the Celebrity Theater, was called Trans-American Video, or TAV. I was able to make a deal to rent the space and get Merv a great little theater that he loved working in. The show was broadcast live from Hollywood.

Even though we were a tremendous hit at the Celebrity Theater, TAV wasn't doing well. Sammy may have been the owner, but he was really just a figurehead. A guy named McClanahan was actually in charge, and he was bilking Sammy and running the business into the ground. They were spending money on limos, fabulous furniture, and tons of office space, with very little to show for it. It was pretty tragic to see. Meanwhile, Sammy's accountant was a phony, so he didn't know how bad things were getting. When McClanahan saw how well Merv and I were doing, he told us he was going to increase our rent. He threw out a number so high that it would have been impossible for us to continue producing the show.

Merv was upset, and I didn't know what to do. Since I'd made the decision to shoulder it all, I couldn't go back to Metromedia and tell them we needed more money.

I started doing some research. I learned that TAV didn't own the building. It was in probate—and for a million dollars it could be ours. Then we wouldn't have to worry about those shady TAV guys and their sky-high rents.

I told Merv about my idea.

"What good is it if we own the building?" he asked.

"Just watch," I told him. With his go-ahead, I bought it.

When it was time for me to go back to McClanahan and let him know whether we'd accept the new rent, I was almost giddy. "So," McClanahan said, "do you accept the increase?"

"We can't make the deal," I said. "It's just too much."

"Well, then, you're out."

"No," I replied, "you're out. We own the building." It was that simple.

Soon after, I met with Sammy to discuss the possibility of buying TAV entirely. We met at the Bacchanal Room at Caesars Palace. The place was empty, but we moved to a table on the side.

"Murray," Sammy said, "don't hurt me."

"I'm not going to hurt you," I told him. "I'm going to make the best deal I can for me, but I'm also going to get you out of debt." With that deal done, we owned TAV and half of Vine Street. It was the best piece of real estate in Hollywood, and it was pretty clever of me to snag it, if I do say so myself.

Now that we owned the theater, I could do whatever I wanted with it. I put a lot of dough into redesigning it. There were brown velvet walls, gold finishes. It would have fit in perfectly on the Vegas Strip. I also had the staff uniforms done by a fashion designer.

One day I came in to find a heavy, unattractive woman at the front desk. Her beautiful uniform was straining at the seams.

"Who put her there?" I whispered to Merv.

"I did," he said.

"She can't be there," I said. "She's ruining the whole look of the place. Put her in the back." It was sexist, yes, but I knew that business was all about appearances, and I wasn't about to disrupt that. Plus, it was a different time. So much of what happened back then would never fly today—in fact, that particular decision was borderline problematic even then.

"We can't do that," Merv said. "We'll get sued."

"Just tell her she's better off doing scheduling." With that, the decision was made. Merv and I were the board—we didn't have to run it by anyone. There was a wonderful simplicity to the way we operated. I came up with an idea, discussed it with Merv, and he would say, "Gee, sounds great. Are you OK with it?" Next, I'd call the lawyer and we'd make the deal. We couldn't do anything like that now. Meanwhile, I hired this adorable blonde gal to be the receptionist instead. Today, she's the supervising producer of *Jeopardy!*

When we were starting Merv Griffin Enterprises, Merv and I had a great working relationship. He had total and absolute trust in me—and he had every reason to. *Jeopardy!* was on the air, and we were in the process of selling *Wheel of Fortune*. "Look," he said, "I do the show, and you take care of business." He respected my role, and he was pretty generous about offices. "My office is the stage," he said. "You're the president and CEO; you take the impressive office." Both of our offices were lovely, but mine was the corner office. It was bigger, more stately, with its own terrace.

I was also committed to looking the part of a CEO-level executive. LA is a casual city—everyone is laid-back. Merv loved wearing these velour warm-up suits, which were trendy at the time, and tennis shoes. Meanwhile, I never came to work without a shirt and tie—it was that old William Morris training—and he admired that. He said, "You're the only guy in this whole building who wears shirts and ties."

"Well," I said, "when you go downstairs to the stage—your office—*you* dress up. This is my stage." And when I began hiring vice presidents, I made sure they adopted the same dress code I'd learned at William Morris. Soon I wasn't the only guy in a suit and tie.

Every morning, Merv would come and sit in one of two chairs in front of my beautiful desk and put his feet up. I hated when he did that—perhaps because it reminded me of being a little fish in the big William Morris pond. But I didn't know what to say, so I lived with it.

But then I had an idea. I called our carpenter and asked him to cut two inches off the legs of the chairs, so that when he sat in front of my desk, I would be much higher than he was. Everyone knew what I had done but Merv—he never caught on.

We were pals. Almost daily, we'd go to lunch at Musso & Frank and discuss business, the show, and my next deal. At night, when the show taped, all the guys would come into my office. I had a bar in it—just like they did in *Mad Men*. In the evenings, the secretaries would bring in ice buckets and cigars and we'd all hang out there.

One night, I had a date coming, a girl from Vegas. We were planning to go out for dinner after the show, so I invited her to join the guys and me in my office, where I'd be hanging out with a group that included a guy named Ross, one of my vice presidents. He was a classic guy; he drove a Cadillac and loved to smoke cigars. Merv hated him. He thought Ross was really sloppy, leaving a trail of ash wherever he went. But I thought he was terrific. He was smart and helpful and I just liked him.

That night, he and I were schmoozing with all the other guys when in walks my gorgeous date from Vegas. Ross asked, "Honey, would you like a drink?"

"Oh yes," my date replied. "I'd love to have a banana daiquiri."

"A banana daiquiri? We don't have fucking bananas here. This is an office. You want a scotch, a bourbon?" Today, we'd probably be accused of harassment for that, and to avoid it, I'd probably have sent out for a banana daiquiri, or I wouldn't have had her meet me at work in the first place. Back then, though, it really was boys being boys, and in our offices, we did what we wanted.

Because we owned the theater, I could also do something else: I could rent it out and pull in a profit. When *The Merv Griffin Show* was away, I could loan the space out so that other shows and specials could film there. The first renter we had was *Entertainment Tonight*, and eventually the Celebrity Theater became the hottest post-production theater in town. All of my training as an agent was paying off. I'd gotten great at maneuvering my way through deals, and I loved doing it.

I figured that if I could rent out the space to different productions, we could go other places too—Monte Carlo, Venice . . . wherever. I also found another way to make even more dough: product placement. Owning the whole package—everything above and below the line—meant we also got advertising dollars, and there was a lot of opportunity to bring those dollars in. We were pioneers of product placement. When you watch *America's Got Talent* and everyone onstage is drinking out of Dunkin' Donuts cups, that's product placement—and we invented it.

It came about that I decided we should bring the show to Vegas. Back when we were at CBS I'd tried to do the same thing, but CBS didn't want me to go through with it. They thought Vegas was bawdy and tacky, that it would debase the quality of the show.

"Wait a minute! Vegas is a family place, and we're going to do a family show," I told them. Of course, Vegas had a lot more illicit activity going on then than it does today, but I wasn't about to tell that to CBS. Plus, I had an ulterior motive. Rumors were starting to circulate that Merv was gay. While most guys in that era wanted to hang out with pretty ladies, especially guys in show business, Merv hung out with a lot of good-looking blond fellows—actor types. They went to dinner, and he'd throw big parties for them at his house.

Regardless of what he was up to, we couldn't have that—it was a different time, and a rumor like that could have been his undoing. So I employed a tactic I'd learned at the Red Mill: I surrounded him with beautiful women. I knew viewers wouldn't see anything else. And there was no better place to do that than Vegas, with its ample supply of dancers and showgirls.

Plus, Hilton agreed to pay us $100,000 for the week, just to be there. The idea was that the company would pay us to be there for publicity purposes—if *The Merv Griffin Show* shot there, it would bring positive attention to Hilton Hotels, and viewers would be influenced to stay there. In other words, more product placement.

We wouldn't have been able to afford to do it otherwise, but $100,000 was enough to cover the below-the-line costs necessary to bring the show to Vegas.

Still, CBS was nervous about it. "Don't screw it up, Murray," they told me. It was a smash hit.

Of course, when the show was canceled, going to Vegas wasn't really an option anymore. But once I had the reins, I could make it happen again. I called Caesars Palace and told them I wanted to make a long-term deal to bring the show there. I was negotiating with tough guys, the same ones who'd invited me to meet with them at one in the morning, rather than one in the afternoon. But Jerry Zarowitz, who ran Caesars, loved the idea. By two or three in the morning, he agreed that *The Merv Griffin Show* would run out of their theater for ten weeks that year. We were celebrating over drinks when he asked when I'd be paying them.

"Pay you? I thought you were paying me."

There was another guy at the table by the name of Sid Gathrid. He had worked for a newspaper in Philadelphia back in the day and understood the importance of promotion.

"No, Jerry," he said. "This kid's giving you a great deal. You're going to be on the air for ninety minutes. That kind of press is priceless."

I wrote the details on a napkin: Caesars Palace would get the invaluable benefit of *The Merv Griffin Show* being "live from Caesars Palace," and we would get $50,000 per week for ten weeks of shows. It would eventually evolve to be a fifteen-year deal, but I wrote the details of the first arrangement on a napkin. Merv came up with cute ideas for how we'd talk about the hotel during the show—how many eggs they used in a day, how many loaves of bread, who does the costuming for the showgirls—and we were in business.

Metromedia was concerned that by doing product placement, we were advertising another company, so I read the FCC rules. It looked to me like the only thing that counted was disclosure, and they agreed. Our lawyer, Roy Blakeman, came up with language you're likely familiar with today: "Promotional payment has been paid for and provided by the following companies . . . ."

One day, Sid Gathrid and I had a disagreement. Our first shows weren't filling the 1,500-seat theater, and without a full turnout, he felt Caesars might be paying us too much. Merv was concerned that viewers would see those empty seats. So I hired some stand-ins to camp out in front of Caesars the night before and got a friend from the *Vegas Sun* to do me a favor and print a photo of the crowd on the front page. I had to pack the theater on the regular, selling folks who wouldn't have wanted to see a TV show in Vegas on the fact that it was free.

I also knew that the people who attended the show would be ushered into an area filled with slot machines while they were waiting to be seated, so I told Sid I'd be willing to consider reducing our weekly fee in exchange for the difference in slot income generated by our audience. He did some research on just how much that would be and decided he was happy with our fee. He also became very generous, offering us all kinds of perks.

After all that, Vegas ended up being a great family place. During the weeks when the show taped in Vegas, we'd finish work on Friday, and I'd have the kids come down for the weekend. Everyone at Caesars was really nice to them, and they'd enjoy the pool, Circus Circus, and other fun places—they never saw the inside of a casino. It was a terrific way to spend time with them.

Finding ways to entertain them also inspired me. At one of the Circus Circus shows, there was a duck in an enclosure. You'd feed a quarter into a machine attached to the side of the enclosure, and the duck would begin to dance. It was amazing to watch. I immediately called Merv. "What an act!" I told him. "Circus Circus has a duck that dances."

"Let's bring it on," he said.

At the show's rehearsal, the duck's trainer showed up and put the duck on a stand we'd built. Everyone was watching, waiting for something to happen, but the duck just stood there. "No, no," I said, feeling a little embarrassed. "He needs music. He dances, I promise. He just needs music." The band began playing the tune the duck had danced to at Circus Circus, but the duck just kept standing there.

Merv started laughing. "Is this another one of your great guests?" He asked. Not long before, I'd booked twelve beautiful Hungarian violinists who were just awful.

"I'm telling you, the duck dances," I insisted. At that point, I was very embarrassed. I went over to the trainer. "Will you get the duck to dance, please."

"He'll dance, he'll dance," the trainer assured me. "You've just got to turn it on."

"Turn what on?" I asked.

"The hot plate." Back at Circus Circus, when you put in a quarter, a hot plate beneath the duck would heat up. That's what made him dance.

"I can't believe it," Merv said, and the act ended right there. They used to do terrible things with animals in those days—it's certainly one aspect of show business that has changed for the better.

* * *

Now that I knew how to do product placement, I could do it anywhere, and with anything. When we went to Monte Carlo, Merv thought it was hilarious that everything appeared on the show—a tennis racket, a can of tennis balls, a special warm-up suit—came with a paycheck. All of the companies behind those products were paying us; we were even being paid by Monte Carlo itself. We were just raking it in.

Things were going so well. There was talk about the company growing, and I wanted to bring it public, eventually. I thought it would be a good idea to own the rest of the property on Vine—the bottom half in addition to the upper half, which we already had. That way, if we were to go public, we'd have our own theater *and* our own post-production center. At the time, it was owned by this guy named Larry Wroschel, who would eventually become one of my dearest friends. I took him to dinner and told him I wanted to buy the rest of the property. "I want ten million," he said.

Well, hey, I thought. *I bought the other property for a million dollars, so the whole block would only be $11 million in total.* It seemed fair enough, and I didn't want to lose the deal by trying to negotiate, so I told him we'd do it.

At Larry's engagement party years later, Larry's partner said, "You know what? Larry would have taken less than ten million."

"I would have paid him more," I told him. Whenever we hung out, we would kid about that.

Merv and I made a great team. I was hungry and desperate. I needed to build something, and he let me. He gave me the latitude to do it, and for that I'll always be grateful.

* * *

One day, Jimmy Blue Eyes came up to see me at our building at Hollywood and Vine. Merv was shocked. Everyone was. There he was, Jimmy Blue Eyes, sitting on my couch in a tennis sweater, older after two stints in prison, and no longer the kingmaker in Florida and Las Vegas. But he was still a made man, one of the toughest crime figures in history, and he'd been an important player in my years with George. Jimmy came to see me as a sign of respect—respect for me, and for what I'd done for George all those years ago, taking care of him and the boys.

Jimmy was very proud of me. (It must sound strange that one of the heads of the Mafia was proud of a guy like me, but it made me glow nonetheless.) I enjoyed showing him what I'd become and how well I'd done, and I gave him a tour of our studios. Merv pulled me aside and said nervously, "Are you going to be hanging around with this guy, Murray?"

"No. He's just visiting from my boyhood." I was able to show Jimmy that I hadn't taken his road or George's. I'd become the president of a big production company, in a large office, with three assistants. Thank you, George. And thanks were due to Jimmy too, for taking me with him around town—to Dinty Moore's, and to Rumplemayer's for tea sandwiches.

CHAPTER 13

The Wrong Place
at the Wrong Time

Then the day came when I was in the wrong place at the wrong time. A hundred things might have been different, but they weren't. And this time, rather than miss the splashy event, as I had when I'd arrived at the scene of Albert Anastasia's murder minutes after the hit had taken place, I fell right into one of the biggest news stories of the decade.

It was June 1976, a couple of weeks before America's bicentennial on July 4, and we'd been taping the *Merv Griffin Celebrity Tennis Tournament* in Monaco, as a fundraiser to support Princess Grace's charity. We'd had a great time, and after Monte Carlo, Merv and the staff went on to England to watch the Wimbledon tennis tournament. I didn't go with them. Instead, I went looking for Big Red, a dancer from Vegas, so I could take her to Greece. I figured I'd have more fun with her in Athens than at a stuffy tennis tournament in England.

Ever since I'd slipped away from the Bronx as a kid to wander the galleries of the Metropolitan Museum, I've liked hanging out in places with rich cultures. To be able to see art and antiquities in their historical sites was a thrill that never paled for me. I remember lazing on the steps of the Parthenon, thinking about how far I'd come from Jerome Avenue and the basement of the Red Mill, gluing photos to matchbook covers. It was a journey of a million miles.

Soon, however, it was time to meet up with Merv again, so I said goodbye to Big Red and booked a flight for Paris. The plan was to meet him for dinner to catch up and talk over our plans for the next year's worth of shows. How could we outdo ourselves? What new territory could we explore?

Air France Flight 139 originated in Tel Aviv. Athens was a stopover on the way to Paris. The flight departed at 12:30 p.m. on June 27. From the moment I boarded, I felt something was wrong. There was no security in Athens. I was in first class and could see every passenger getting on, passing me on the way back to the coach section. More than one had lumps under their jackets and held bulky packages. I thought, *Oh, what the hell*, and took the customary glass of champagne they offered.

As the plane was ascending, a blonde German woman burst out of the first class bathroom holding two grenades. I think she must have hidden there before takeoff. "Everyone sit!" she shouted.

As a New Yorker, I've seen my fair share of crazies, and my first thought was, *Don't make eye contact with her. She's nuts.* So I did what I'd always done on the subway when someone who appeared to be a little goofy entered my car. I looked away and kept drinking that glass of champagne. (Well, the looking away part I did on the subway. Even *I* don't drink champagne underground.)

But I wasn't riding a train from the Bronx to Manhattan. I was aboard a plane that was climbing to 30,000 feet. "Sit!" screamed the woman with the grenades.

"I *am* sitting," says Mr. Smartass. Next thing I knew, a man from the back of the plane entered first class and stuck a gun in my ribs, shouting at me, "Back, back! Go to the back of the plane!" By now I understood what was happening here, and as the terrorists took over the first class cabin, I thought, *I'm going to get killed on this plane.*

My flight had been hijacked by the Popular Front for the Liberation of Palestine (PFLP), which had pulled off other hijackings in the past. This time they added two German revolutionaries, Brigitte Kuhlmann and Wilfried Böse. It was Kuhlmann who held the grenades. *This is it,* I thought. *This is how it ends for me.*

I went to the back of the plane and sat on the floor while the terrorists collected our passports. They then closed all the blinds so we couldn't see where we were going.

The hijackers began rifling through my things. In my traveling bag, I had a letter from Princess Grace thanking me for my work at the television event, detailing all the ways in which I'd contributed to the success of the evening. My captors found the letter. "What is this? Why do you have a letter from Princess Grace?" they asked.

"I supply and repair home entertainment systems. I did that for Grace Kelly in America before she became a princess," I told them. I didn't want them to know that they had an executive on their hands, someone who'd be seen as a high-value target. For that very reason, I'd already shoved my business cards down the toilet, blocking it up. Fortunately, they bought my excuse. Those Jerome Avenue and Red Mill street smarts came in handy high above the Mediterranean Sea.

I also drew on the other skills I'd honed over the course of my career. Those years with George, Jimmy Blue Eyes, and the boys had taught me to hide my feelings well. When George screamed at me, I didn't react. I could always read him. He used to purse his lips and shake his head from side to side when he was thinking hard. When he pursed his lips and nodded, that was anger. I knew when hell was coming: when he nodded his head up and down, I knew he was about to blow. Those expressions are still so vivid for me. But George the seasoned gambler couldn't read me. He never knew what I was thinking until I chose to say what was on my mind.

I felt I'd better not ever let George or the boys see me scared, so I showed them that I was willing to stand up to their crap. These were tough guys, and I think they respected my *apparent* lack of fear. From those experiences, I knew I could keep a cool head, and I knew that would be helpful to me in this situation. So I took on a leadership role.

I pulled out a map and said, "Given the direction the plane is headed, I think we're going to Red China," which was pretty stupid, if you think about it.

"That's good," said the other passengers. "The Chinese will negotiate."

For the duration of that long flight, we felt comforted. China wouldn't harbor terrorists holding American captives.

Hours later we landed and I opened one of the window shades just a sliver, so our captors wouldn't notice. This was against the rules, but I did it anyway. I'm a negotiator, and to negotiate from a position of strength, one has to know what's happening on both sides of the table.

Instead of approaching an arrivals gate in Shanghai or Beijing, though, the plane taxied past an Arab sitting on a camel, holding a gun. So much for China—we'd landed in Benghazi, Libya. How strange history is, connecting dots and adding meaning across distant eras. We sat on the ground in Benghazi for seven hours. While we were there, we refueled, but more important, the terrorists let off a pregnant British-born Israeli woman who appeared to be having a miscarriage.

We waited in Benghazi, with no way of knowing what would happen next. My nerves began to fray. This was no place to be with the last name Schwartz.

Eventually, we took off again and were told that we were headed to Uganda. Now, I knew about Idi Amin and his brutality. In the US we'd heard he was a cannibal. Many years later, when a reporter for the *New York Times* asked Amin about the rumor, rather than deny it, he said, "I don't like human flesh. It's too salty for me." Very funny, but not far outside the realm of possibility. This was a man who'd thrown his own ministers to the crocodiles in Lake Victoria, and we were about to be delivered to him like a package.

We existed minute by minute. I thought about my children; I was grateful they weren't with me to experience this, but also afraid I'd never see them again. I remembered the day I'd won custody of Jenny and had rushed to the plane that would take her home with me to LA. What a different flight that had been.

The plane landed at Entebbe Airport in Uganda, the aircraft door was opened, and there stood Idi Amin and his young son, still a child, in matching military uniforms. Amin was known primarily for the mass executions of his so-called enemies, mostly the Christian tribes that had been loyal to his predecessor. We were taken off the plane and brought to the airport, where we were led into a hangar. Then we were herded into the transit hall of the old airport. Four more terrorists joined the four from the plane, and Amin's troops backed up our eight captors. At this point the plane was blown up—with everything on it, including our luggage.

The transit hall was run-down, and to separate us by nationality, the terrorists broke through one of the walls to an empty room, creating a second holding area. Hostages with Israeli passports, including those with dual nationality, were put into one room, and the rest of us were put into the other.

One of the Jewish passengers was a Holocaust survivor and showed Böse, the male German terrorist, the registration number tattooed on his arm. Böse said, "I'm no Nazi. I'm an idealist." What ideals could they possibly have been peddling?

I stuck my head of the window of the airport hangar. The jungle that surrounded the airport was dense, green, and dark, despite the midday sun. Even if I made it across the tarmac and away from the airport buildings without being shot, the jungle would find a way to kill me, quickly. I inhaled. The air was hot and heavy and smelled like nothing I've ever smelled before—acrid, like something burning. Rubber? Vegetation? I couldn't tell.

Time crept by. Inside the rooms where we were being held, a malaise began to replace the fear of being hijacked high above Athens on an Air France jet bound for Paris. Without any real inkling of what was happening outside the hangar, we found ourselves fighting despair.

Through the window, I could see guards carrying machine guns, which hung across their chests on thick straps. The crease made on the gunmen's shirts by the straps seemed familiar. My memory flicked on, like the tube of an old television set, and I could see a similar strap slung across my own young chest—my shirt and jacket creased just like that of the kid I now watched pacing across the baking African ground.

It wasn't a gun at the end of my strap, though. It was a mailbag, and I was seventeen years old, delivering mail to important men in the William Morris office in New York City. That seemed like a lifetime ago.

The sun poured through an open window, and its warmth on my face was soothing. I looked down at my arms, appreciating my new tan, but just for a moment. The pressure of the gun that had been stuck into my side a few days before had left a painful, purple bruise. I lifted my shirt to examine it, worrying that I'd broken a rib. Then I went back to daydreaming about those first years at William Morris.

"What are you thinking about?" said a voice behind me. It was Cynthia, one of the other hostages. Like me, she was from New York, and in the middle of her life.

"Rumplemayer's," I said. "I could really go for a vanilla milkshake right now."

"What I wouldn't give for a cold, dry martini," she responded.

I turn my face back toward the window. "How did I get here?" I wondered out loud. I had left Monte Carlo in a tuxedo, and here I was sitting on the floor of an airport in Uganda.

Have you ever wondered how you arrived in a particular moment? Usually that moment is a crisis, a point you think might have been avoided, if only you'd taken a different turn somewhere, anywhere, sooner. But where? And what else might you have lost along the way if you'd made that choice?

I wasn't thinking solely of a holding room in Uganda. I was thinking of my first class seat on the Air France plane taking me from Athens to Paris. How did I get to the life in which first class was the norm, its endless glasses of champagne standard? I was such a long way from the mailroom, and even farther from the Red Mill. Maybe

I was never meant to be there in the first place, to be Mr. Schwartz in that first class seat.

Regardless, my principles hadn't changed much over the course of my life, and something was bothering me. The hijacking had forced me to stand Merv up. He was in Paris waiting for me when my flight took off. I never stood anyone up. It was a serious breach of my social code, and I wanted to get home to make it up to him. I wanted to see him sitting across from me in my office, his chair just low enough that he had to stretch a little bit to swing his legs up over my desk. I wouldn't even mind those dirty tennis shoes on the beautifully polished wood. Home. Would I ever make it back there?

I knew there was only so much I had control over, but I was determined to manage what little I could. I only drank coffee, because I knew the water had been boiled, though eventually I stopped doing that too—I didn't trust the filthy urn they'd made it in. I wouldn't eat the meat that was given to us either. Even though it was cooked, it was green. I'd scrubbed mold off my fair share of chickens at the Red Mill, but this was not the Bronx, and I had to be very careful to survive. Getting sick wouldn't have served me. So I ate only bananas, rice, and whatever vegetables I could peel—it was the closest you could get to organic at the time. Thanks to this diet, I lost weight in captivity. I must say, between my slimmer frame and my deep tan, I looked good.

On the second day, the terrorists made their demands known. The release of fifty-three Palestinian and pro-Palestinian militants, forty of whom were prisoners in Israel, would secure *our* release. They also wanted $5 million. If these demands weren't met, the terrorists would begin to kill hostages on July 1.

On the fourth day, forty-seven sick and elderly hostages, and all the mothers with children, were released from the non-Israeli group and flown to Paris. Dora Bloch, a seventy-four-year-old grandmother, was taken to a hospital in Kampala after choking on some food. She was never heard from again, and we later learned she'd passed away. She was one of four fatalities among the passengers.

We didn't know that Israel was negotiating behind the scenes. I thought it was all over. While we were being held in Uganda, I became friendly with Cynthia Zeger, the woman who'd asked what I was thinking about during that first day. Her son was Erich Segal, author of the best-selling novel *Love Story*. I was certain I'd be killed, but I figured they might let the women go. So I wrote a farewell letter to Suzy and Jenny and gave it to Cynthia to deliver to my kids.

Idi Amin visited us daily, hosting news conferences from our holding area. It was surreal. He kept promising he would free us through negotiations. There are newsreels of those news conferences, and I've heard that I can be seen in them, sticking my head into the frame. The hostages were with Amin when he spoke before news cameras, and like Zelig, I was there, making sure I was visible. I didn't want to disappear.

Thanks to that footage, Merv and everyone at home could see that I was all right. My daughters were at home with their nanny, Merv's wife, and Susan Stafford. Merv had flown back to Paris from England at the end of Wimbledon to meet me for dinner, and instead waited to learn of my fate as a hostage. He was ready to put up a million dollars or more in ransom money. It never came to that, but I never forgot it.

Later on, I'd learn about all that had happened during that terrifying week. At first, Israel's cabinet agreed—against their policy—to negotiate with the hijackers and release some, but not all, of the Arab prisoners. But that wasn't enough for our captors. It was all or nothing. In the airport, as diplomatic solutions began to dry up, we felt our options were also evaporating—though we didn't know what our captors wanted. I remember when they started calling out the Jewish last names. They passed "S" and didn't call me. I realized then that they wanted Israeli citizens, not merely Jews. This was a fight over territory, not religious differences. Even so, I had a glimpse of what it must have been like during the Holocaust: "You to the left, you to the right."

Still, no one was exempt from the danger of it all. The whole place was ringed with dynamite. They told us to get into the center yard and lined us up. I remember deciding to walk to the front. If I was going to be killed, I wanted to get it over with fast. My worry was that if I stood in the back, I would only be wounded—that the end would be much more painful and drawn out.

My humor never waned, though. One of the most bizarre things I did was wash my underwear. After we were taken off the plane and it was blown up with our luggage still on it, we were left with nothing but the clothes we were wearing when we'd boarded. After four days I needed to do something to feel better. I was wearing a pair of striped nylon briefs that had been perfect for Monte Carlo, but not that great for a hijacking. Given the quick-drying properties of nylon, though, I thought they'd dry quickly if I could rinse them in the sink.

A large Ugandan woman guarded the men's room; I stripped down in front of her and stood there naked, washing the underwear in the sink. There was actually a clothesline for the hostages on which we could hang our things to dry. As I walked out of the bathroom, two of the captors saw the bikini underwear I was about to pin to the line. "Faggot," they called me—not very politically correct, but that's what they said.

So Mr. Bronx said, "Go fuck yourself."

"Come here," they said.

They tied a grenade to my head and attached the pin to a string. Then I was made to walk around a small yard near the perimeter of the hangar repeating, "I'm sorry." It seemed an appropriate time to apologize, so I did what they asked, walking in circles saying, "I'm sorry," until I became faint. At any point one of them could have pulled the string and detonated the grenade.

Was I scared? Of course I was. I was sure my life would end at any given moment.

And then I was released. The Americans and women were let go. One of our guards was a seventeen-year-old kid. I'd been taking loads of photos, and before I was released the kid took the film out of the camera. We just stared at each other, then said goodbye.

My fellow hostages had grown close too. In fact, two of the hostages fell in love. One night, I'd looked up to see them under a blanket, the man on top and the woman below. He was moving back and forth. *There's only one thing they could be doing*, I thought.

I didn't know how he could even think about sex at a time like that. I was pretty wild back then too, spending plenty of nights in the company of dancers and showgirls, but in that dilapidated airport, with the constant threat of death hanging over my head, sex was the last thing on my mind. *He must be a pretty horny guy*, I said to myself. Meanwhile, she was lying there with just the hard floor beneath her, just taking it—talk about being on your back.

Who knows what goes on in people's heads? Situations like that do strange things to people. Maybe they were thinking, *We may never get another chance; they could kill us any minute.* I remember how they held each other on the plane going home, like they'd never let go.

It was rumored among the hostages that one of our captors was the famed terrorist the Jackal. It was thought that he'd masterminded the hijacking and had been held with us before being smuggled out with the rest of the hostages. There were even hints that he was one of the people who fell in love in captivity. That was the rumor, anyway. I never learned what happened to that couple.

Upon our release, we learned that Air France had dispatched another plane to take us from Uganda to Kenya. There I met the German ambassador, who arranged our flight to France. We didn't know what was going on, but now that freedom seemed imminent, I wasn't about to take any chances and get lost or kidnapped again. I wouldn't even use the men's room by myself. I said to the German ambassador, "I'm staying next to you. I'm not leaving you for one minute, pal. If anything, I'm going to hold hands with you as we leave."

He got a kick out of me. He said, "You're free to walk around; it's an airport."

I said, "*You* walk around the airport, but I'm not leaving your side."

When I arrived in Paris, Merv was waiting for me. He was very assertive about getting my story out and had arranged for *The Today Show* to cover my arrival. Merv got my children on the phone, securing an open line from *The Today Show*. He called my daughters and said, "Your dad's home; he made it."

"Hey, Murray, could I have an exclusive on this story?" Merv asked a little later.

"Maybe that would be OK, let me think about it," I replied, kidding with him.

A photo of me getting off the plane from Kenya ended up on the front page of the *Los Angeles Times* in a full-page story that recounted the whole experience. The hijacking was big news across the globe, and as a result, so was I. For a time, I was a hero at cocktail parties. The story became embellished to the point that I practically became one of the commandos.

As soon as I'd talked to my children, Mossad grabbed me and took me away to be debriefed. They wanted to know how many terrorists there were, what kind of planes they had, how many guns there'd been and what type. The planes were Soviet MiGs, I remember. I was able to give complete details about the layout of the airport, the positions of the guards, and where the remaining hostages were being held. One would've thought the terrorists would assume the freed hostages would provide information that would make a raid upon the terrorists possible, but it seemed more important to them to free the Americans, so as not to have to take on the United States. The Ugandans seemed willing to take on the Israelis, but not to try to fight the Americans.

Our cooperation gave the Israelis the intel they needed. That's when Israel began planning a military operation. They worked the details out on Friday night—Shabbat. Thirty-five commandos would arrive by plane dressed in Ugandan uniforms. They would drive out of the belly of the plane in three vehicles, including a Mercedes flying the Ugandan flag to make it look official. The idea was that the soldiers' garb and vehicles would suspend the guards' suspicion for long enough to allow the Israeli soldiers to make it to the airport.

At one point, they thought about having one soldier pose as Idi Amin himself, who was supposed to be getting back from a meeting in Mauritius, but they scrapped that plan when he came back to Uganda early. Then they thought about making up the commandos in blackface to help them blend in with the Ugandan soldiers, but they decided against it, figuring that it could confuse the Israeli commandos as to who the real targets were. Plus, it was so dark out there that one probably couldn't tell the difference from a distance anyway.

The commandos would then enter the airport and head to the holding rooms where the remaining hostages were being kept, while a second group would descend on the Ugandan soldiers camped out on the second floor. Yet another group would protect the planes slotted to carry the hostages back to Israel.

Two days later, they carried out their plan. The raid took place on July 4, 1976. One hundred elite Israeli commandos were flown to Uganda under the cover of darkness. A gun battle ensued, killing the hijackers and as many as forty-five Ugandan soldiers. The commandos also destroyed all the Russian-built MiGs on the ground, thus preventing them from attacking the Israeli aircrafts when they left the airport. They were able to rescue the hostages—most of them Israeli—and rush them into three waiting American-supplied C-130 Hercules jet transporters and fly them to Israel via Nairobi.

There were a few losses, though. The Israeli elite unit's commander, Lt. Colonel Yoni Netanyahu (the older brother of Israel's current prime minister, Benjamin Netanyahu), was the only Israeli killed in the fighting. "Operation Thunderbolt," the mission to free the rest of the hostages, was retroactively renamed "Operation Jonathan" in his honor. Meanwhile, Amin retaliated against Kenya for cooperating with the Israelis by killing 245 Kenyans who were living in Uganda, including the airport staff at Entebbe.

In Paris, I bought new clothes and obtained a new passport. All of my belongings had been blown up in Uganda. I celebrated the fact that I was still alive with Merv and friends over champagne and caviar. Merv asked if I'd been afraid. Of course I'd been afraid, but

I never wanted to show fear to anyone. I'd created a certain image for myself—that nothing bothered me—long ago. It wasn't true, but my front worked.

In 2018 I attended a screening of a film on the ordeal, *7 Days in Entebbe*, at the Laemmle Theatres. There'd been other good films on the rescue, but this one was a disaster.

"What did you think of the film?" a woman asked me afterward.

"I thought it was awful, just trash." I told her. "It was totally sympathetic to the hijackers, who were basically Nazis."

"You just didn't understand the plight of the Palestinians," she said. "I've read a lot about this."

"Have you really? Well, the movie wasn't about the plight of the Palestinians; it was about people being hijacked. About people being separated like they did in the war, like they did during the Holocaust."

"You're getting pretty wound up about this," she told me. "Why are you so emotional?"

"I was there. I was on the plane." After that, she didn't have much to say. As I watched her walk away, I thought, *They should have included that couple having sex in the airport. That would have made for a much better movie.*

* * *

After our dramatic rescue, I decided I wanted to know more about Israel, so I proposed to Merv that we do our annual Christmas show there. Without missing a beat, Merv gave me his "wow" look. He was into the idea.

Within days, Prime Minister Yitzhak Rabin—who was later assassinated—arranged for me to meet with his staff at the Israeli Embassy. The Embassy arranged for our transportation and lodging.

They scheduled the events and provided us with a guide. This was in exchange to promote the State of Israel, much like what we'd done on our trips to Monte Carlo and Vegas. Weeks later, *The Merv Griffin Show* was broadcasting from Israel.

Ross Easty, my vice president and unit manager, had worked for a television network before I enlisted him to join Merv Griffin Enterprises. He was an expert on technical requirements, and we flew ahead of the staff to set up for the show.

Merv was impressed that I turned my hijacking into a rave event for *The Merv Griffin* Show, and in his twenty-five years on the air, he believed this week of shows from Israel to be the most meaningful and noble work we'd ever done. We established warm relationships in Israel and made our way around the country. We visited the holiest of all religious sites. We saw the Garden of Gethsemane, where—according to the New Testament—Jesus was arrested the night before his crucifixion. We went to the Wailing Wall, the site of the Second Temple and one of the most sacred locations in Judaism, where Merv donned a yarmulke. We visited the Church of the Holy Sepulchre in the Christian Quarter of the Old City, which is said to be where Jesus was crucified and which houses his empty tomb.

Merv played tennis with Prime Minister Rabin. He interviewed the commandos and survivors of the raid. We taped an Arabian horse race in the Negev Desert. We dined with Arab sheiks, one of whom burped in Merv's face as a compliment.

For a touch of glamour, I arranged for a bikini fashion show at the pool in Tel Aviv. The goal was to show off the beautiful Israeli women. Merv said, "You can take the boy out of the Red Mill, but you can't take the Red Mill out of the boy." Yes, we are shaped by our past.

As we planned for the trip, I learned that Merv had considered studying for the priesthood as a young man. He wanted to sing "A Child Is Born" somewhere, to be broadcast in America on Christmas Eve. He recorded the music in Los Angeles and planned to sing to the track.

In Israel, Ross and I went to Bethlehem, accompanied by heavily armed security, to see if we could have Merv sing in the manger. The Greek Orthodox Church controlled it. When I asked the priest if Merv could sing there, he refused, saying they needed authorization from the Vatican for something like that.

"We're doing a show later today," I explained. "We don't have time." Then I took all the petty cash Ross had on hand and offered it to the priest as a donation. With that, he gave us the go-ahead. The manger, or Grotto of the Nativity, didn't look at all like we were expecting. We found ourselves entering a rock cave, with a very low door built to prevent horses from entering back in the day. Merv performed the song with dignity and sensitivity, in a manner fit for such a spiritual place.

That day, there was a group of nuns visiting the Holy Land. They heard the music drifting up from the grotto below. They thought they were witnessing some kind of miracle. To this day, I've never heard of anyone—including a religious figure—having done what Merv did there. I haven't heard of anyone else doing an entertainment show from Israel either. We brought awareness to that wonderful little bastion of democracy in a dangerous neighborhood. When I think about it, it really was a miracle.

The Israeli government bestowed honors on us for our contributions. This time I was on the front page of the Israeli newspapers: "Hostage on Flight 139 Brings American Television to Israel." The

William Morris Agency had taught me to make deals, and I loved every part of this one.

In Israel, I met Lt. Gen. Mordechai Gur, chief of staff for the Israeli Defense Forces (IDF). It was Lt. Gen. Gur who'd planned and executed Operation Jonathan. We talked about the event. I told him I was sorry that the boy who'd guarded me was killed in the raid, and Gur said, "Don't you feel anything for him. He was trained to kill you." I couldn't help it, though. I understood the impact of life's conditions on decisions and behavior more than most.

Looking back, I think I got through the experience in one piece thanks to the lessons I learned by living a complex life. Negotiation skills are very useful, even outside of business. I've seen that time and again. And though this situation was more extreme than anything I'd ever been through before—though all of it unfolded in the jungle rather than in a boardroom or a chic restaurant—those skills were just as pertinent, if not more so.

Over the course of my life, I've been grateful to George for a number of reasons. The early imprint he made on me was a crucial factor in my survival both in business and when it came to life and death. In an offhand manner, the sense of style he helped me cultivate even played a role in helping me make it out of there alive—it gave me confidence in the heat of the crisis.

After the hijacking I was interviewed by Rona Barrett, a famous gossip columnist of the day—her work was a combination of TMZ and *Inside Edition*. She asked me to describe the worst moment of the ordeal. I didn't want to make it a tearjerker—that doesn't work for me, it's just not my style—so I said, "Well, the very worst thing was that Idi Amin ended up wearing my cuff links and my Gucci loafers."

Later, Rona got us out of a jam. I got to know her well enough that when I heard she might be working on a story about Merv being gay, I simply walked over to her office and asked her not to. She acquiesced.

When her book, *Miss Rona*, came out, she signed my copy. *Dear Murray,* she wrote. *Thanks for being so good n' gutsy. Love, Rona.*

I also made good on my promise to Merv, sharing my story on *The Merv Griffin Show*. At that point, I was getting a lot of press, and during the show Merv asked me, "Who's going to play your part in the movie?"

"Helen Hayes," I answered, naming one of the greatest leading ladies of the twentieth century. I delivered the line perfectly, without missing a beat. That got one of the biggest laughs on the show. There's a picture of Merv and me on the set of *The Merv Griffin Show* from that night, laughing together. In the shot, we look like brothers having a great time.

Walter Matthau was the next guest, and he made a comment about me too. "What an interesting guy," he said. Merv glossed right over it. Merv and I were certainly pals, but there was a strange tension developing between us—and I believe it was because he was living a lie.

CHAPTER 14

"Why Don't You Call Me Chief?"

Around the time we traveled to Monte Carlo, right before the hijacking, Merv began to change. We'd become rich and successful, and that brought out a side of Merv I hadn't seen before. Money works like a magnifying glass on your character. If you take a miserable guy and give him money, he'll be a miserable guy with money. If you take a happy guy and give him money, he'll be a much happier guy. Merv fell into the former category.

I can't say for sure, but I think Merv's misery stemmed from the secret he'd kept over the course of his life—at times even from himself. The rumors that had been circulating around Hollywood for years were true: Merv was gay.

Of course, being gay was frowned upon at the time. No one in show business was out back then. Even today, there are plenty of closeted actors who don't dare come out for fear of damaging their careers. Though some of Merv's viewers would've probably been fine with it, there were hordes of aunties and grandmas all over the country with whom that just wouldn't have flown. It would've brought disrepute to the firms paying his salary, and that wouldn't have been acceptable either. So he kept it to himself. But after a while, he grew tired of living that lie, and money couldn't make it better.

Merv had always liked rubbing shoulders with anyone and everyone—it's what made him so lovable to those aunties and grandmas in Memphis and Branson and Kalamazoo. Around that time, though, when success had become par for the course and we were taking *The Merv Griffin Show* around the world, his form of interviewing changed.

The beauty of Merv had always been in his ability to appear awestruck, to put his elbows on the table, gaze into his subjects' eyes, and say, "Wow, really?"—and to mean it when he said it. But eventually, he lost that particular talent.

Whereas our trip to Monte Carlo would have once unlocked a sense of wonder in Merv, he acted as if that visit was nothing. He became more pontifical than awestruck. And he expected everyone around him to buy into the self-importance he began projecting—me included. It began showing up in little ways, moments of tension that arose here and there.

I'd written a letter to Ronald Reagan, telling him what a great leader I thought he was. He sent a kind response, ending the letter with *P.S.: Say "hi" to Merv*. I had the letter framed and hung it in my office. When Merv scanned the letter on my wall, he said, "Hey, I wonder why he calls you Mr. Schwartz and me Merv." I could tell he felt as if he was being disrespected by the president—and worse, that he worried Reagan potentially held me in higher regard than him.

I was dumbfounded by his response. "I guess it's because he's closer to you than he is to me," I ventured. That moment encapsulated the ways in which Merv was changing, and the potential impact of money, fame, and secrets on the human psyche at large.

A lifetime of repressing his sexuality was taking its toll. While he'd become big and important, making more dough than he knew what to do with, it meant zip in terms of allowing him to be his true self. The internal torment he felt started to show, both in the way he interacted with other people and in his physical appearance—he gained a lot of weight.

And then, he met someone.

While he was in Paris waiting for my release from the hijackers, Merv encountered a guy named Brent Plott. In fact, I later found a *Daily News* article describing the Entebbe ordeal. In the photograph, I'm on the phone talking to my kids, a week's worth of stubble on my cheeks. In the background is Plott himself.

After being around for so many years, my instincts told me not to trust him—that he had ulterior motives. I could spot a phony sleazebag from a mile away. And ultimately, in my humble opinion, that's exactly what he would show himself to be.

Brent was young—nearly thirty years younger than Merv. He was good looking and cultured, an American living in Paris full time. He spoke several languages. But he was also known to be a gigolo of sorts, seducing older guys into taking care of him. Merv agreed to do the same, moving Brent into his house in Lake Hollywood and claiming he'd simply hired him to be his bodyguard, all while giving Brent his own room downstairs and the opportunity to live the good life on Merv's dime.

Meanwhile, Brent maintained that he was Merv's business consultant. What did Brent know about business? The same as my beautiful golden retriever Valentina knows: absolutely nothing.

He never had a single job that anyone knew about. I wasn't about to offer up my opinion on him, however. when it came to Brent, I kept my distance. I thought it was best for me to stay aloof and stay away. I didn't want to get involved in whatever was going on between them.

* * *

While Merv never came out—he simply couldn't have done so in those days; there were morals clauses in every contract—he became more overt about his relationship with Brent. When my daughter Suzy got married, Merv brought both his wife and Brent. I have a photograph from that night. In the picture, Merv is seated at a table with Al Krivin, the president of Metromedia. His wife is on one side of him, and Brent is on the other.

Back then, I was shocked that he had brought Brent, particularly because those rumors were ramping up. It seemed as if the *Enquirer* was speculating about Merv's sexuality every other week. But now I can't imagine how hard it must have been for Merv, how badly he must have wanted to have a caring relationship and have it be visible to the world, to have the same privileges everyone else did.

Years later, I got a call from the *Enquirer*. "We'd like to know about this guy Brent," they said. "Merv claims that he's his chauffeur."

Of course, I didn't want to turn against Merv, mostly because of my own integrity. So I said, "Look, I was the president of the company. If you want to know about chauffeurs, I'll give you the name of our limousine company, but I don't know anything about it." Had I wanted to be a creep, I could've simply sent them the photos from the wedding.

Merv's wife, Julann, hung in there for a while, but eventually she couldn't deal with it anymore and they got divorced. Years later, he had Eva Gabor serve as his beard, bringing her to parties and high-profile events, though Brent was always waiting in the wings.

Eva didn't mind at all—she loved being around Merv. He impressed her. They could take trips on the yacht he bought, and that was good enough for her. Their arrangement worked out for him too, of course; not only did she serve as his cover, he could bring Brent along and she didn't care.

But all that secrecy couldn't have ended well. Brent and Merv's relationship would eventually cease, and Brent went on to sue Merv for more than $250 million in "palimony." He claimed he'd been Merv's "companion, confidant, secretary, driver, and personal advisor" for the duration of their relationship, telling the courts—and the rest of the world—that Merv had promised to support him for the rest of his life, and that he was simply suing to get what was rightfully his. [1] He exposed all the intimate details of their relationship to the media, telling NBC News, "We lived together, shared the same bed, same house, same television set."[2]

Merv said he was "outraged that a financially troubled former employee would resort to such an action"[3] (he maintained that Brett was nothing more than a member of his staff—whether it be a bodyguard, chauffeur, stableman, or what have you).

Later, Deney Terrio, the host of *Dance Fever*, sued Merv for $11.3 million, claiming that Merv had sexually harassed him. In an interview for the show *A Current Affair*, Deney claimed Merv attacked him, that he "fell on top of [him] and started grabbing [him]

---

1 "Merv Griffin Sued by 'Pal,'" *The Washington Post*, April 12, 1991.

2 Ibid.

3 Ibid.

and tearing [his] shirt off."[4] His accusations were so demeaning and horrid for Merv.[5]

After those lawsuits, guys who'd had relationships with Merv started coming out of the woodwork. It was blood in the water for a school of sharks. Heaven (and Merv's lawyers) only knows how much he doled out over the years to keep his name and image out of the press. And while he claimed outrage at Plott and Terrio's accusations, more than anything, I believe Merv was sad.

* * *

Merv had always been a loyal guy. There was one time, shortly after I became Merv's agent, when he did a show for President Kennedy. He needed a singer for the show, and he knew what Kennedy was into. I'm sure you do, too: Marilyn Monroe types, or bathing beauties, as we called them back then.

But I had a different idea. I thought Barbra Streisand would be perfect. There was simply no one out there like her. Merv was hesitant, but I persisted, telling him she was the right choice—in his book, he even wrote that I tenaciously pushed for her. Eventually he went along with it, booking her for the occasion. He trusted me—and I was right on. After her performance, the audience went wild. Later on, she stopped the president to ask for his autograph. She'd been instructed not to do so under any circumstances, but Kennedy seemed flattered. Photographers snapped away as he signed his name for her, and the next day, pictures of the two of them were in all of the papers. It was one of my best decisions.

---

4 "'Dance Fever' Host Says Merv Griffin Attacked Him," *The Orlando Sentinel*, January 8, 1992.
5 Ibid.

For years, I never doubted Merv's trust in me. He had always done right by me. But Merv's new attitude also began to put a strain on our relationship. After a while, he was no longer the authentic, empathetic guy willing to give a young agent his first big break and trust his instincts.

I was flying back and forth to Vegas to do business on behalf of *The Merv Griffin Show*. One day, out of nowhere, Merv asked me, "Murray, are you fucking all of the staff?" I didn't know what he meant by it. Was this a test of some sort?

"What do you mean?" I asked.

"All the secretaries," he said. "They sure like hanging around your office."

"Are you kidding me?" I exclaimed. "I've been in Vegas ten weeks a year for the last fifteen years. You think I'm going to fuck a secretary who works *here*?"

In truth, I think the question stemmed from jealousy. I had all the trappings of success, a lovely home in Encino, a beach cottage in the Hamptons, two kids. I had all that, and I still got to have fun. I got to enjoy the fruits of our labor and be a free spirit, making deals and dating beautiful women.

Of course, Merv could have bought any of the stuff I had—a beautiful house, a beach cottage, and more. But all the money in the world couldn't have bought him the freedom to do even one hundredth of the things I could do as a straight person. I think he was jealous of my ability to know who I was and live the way I chose. He had the money—of course he did—but he didn't have the freedom. I had both.

And I was committed to staying true to who I was. I would never kiss his ass the way everyone else did.

All of our staff called him "chief." "Murray, how come you never call me chief?" he asked me one day.

"Because you're not my chief," I told him. "I only have one chief, and that's a higher power than you'll ever be." I said it jokingly, of course, but I also meant it. I could never call another human being "chief." In fact, if God was here right now and he called me "boss," I'd say, "Please don't call me that."

"What should I call you?"

"Mr. Schwartz will be fine," I'd tell Him.

I thought my response to Merv was funny, but he didn't laugh.

When we'd go to Musso & Frank's for lunch—five or six guys, including Merv and me—Merv would say, "Who's having sand dabs?" Everyone else would follow his lead, raising their hand and ordering the same thing.

"Murray, what are you having?" he would ask me.

Now, I love sand dabs as much as the next guy, but at Musso's, I always ordered the chicken salad. I couldn't be swayed by Merv or the herd.

"Me? I'm having the chicken salad," I told him, resting my hands on the menu.

Money, power, connections, even glamour didn't change me. I grew—I became more sophisticated and worldlier, more traveled, more well read. Books like *Man's Search for Meaning* by the psychiatrist Viktor Frankl shaped my worldview. I came to love theater and opera, but then again, I'd always had a deep intellectual curiosity and a taste for culture. In so many ways, I was the same boy who'd left the Red Mill all those years ago. My ego remained the same as it always had been. That wasn't the case for Merv, and I couldn't play along with the rest of the guys and address him the way he wanted, or behave exactly as he prescribed.

Maybe it was my background, seeing my father being demeaned with that terrible nickname I hated for so many years, all while dutifully following the Kayes' every instruction. That became part of the conflict between Merv and me. Perhaps it was part of why he admired me too—that I continued to be an individual and do my own thing when everyone else simply got in line and puckered up.

He knew, too, that even though I wouldn't kiss his ass, I was always fully committed to him. Merv never read a contract. One time he saw me pull up to the office in a new car. "Murray, is that a new Mercedes?" he asked.

"Yeah, I hadn't gotten a new one in a couple of years," I told him.

"Well, a lot of people hold on to their cars for a while. I haven't gotten a new one in a long time."

"Merv, my agreement says I get a new one every year."

"It does?" he asked. He'd never bothered to look at it, because he didn't have to. I always had that sense of right and wrong, a gift from my father I held onto indefinitely.

We had our own codes at the Red Mill. For example, you don't touch the dancers, or the shillelagh will come down on your knuckles—hard. For that reason, I never did anything unscrupulous. I learned from George that being underhanded doesn't serve one in the end. I was impeccably honest, as evidenced by all the years Merv and I worked together, with no lawsuits, no problems—no nothing. When there were any issues, I took care of them. I ran the business side of things, and he depended on me to do that.

I've talked about innocence a lot here—my own, as well as the innocence of the time, but I could be shrewd when the situation called for it. At one point, Merv wrote a book with Peter Barsocchini, an author and screenwriter. He arrived out of nowhere and suddenly became producer of the show, with no background or experience in the industry whatsoever. He would eventually achieve some success, writing *High School Musical* for Disney, which became a multibillion-dollar franchise.

In the book, they wrote about how Sid Luft, Judy Garland's third husband, slapped Judy in the face at a bar once. Sid was a nasty guy, and that pissed him off. He said he would not only sue Merv, but that he would also spread rumors about Merv and Peter. Merv said, "Murray, take care of it." So I went into a meeting with Sid's lawyer. We discussed Sid's claims and his plans to spread rumors about Merv. The lawyer mentioned something about quid pro quo, and then he heard a click.

"What was that noise?" he asked. I'd been recording the whole thing, and I told him so. That was the end of that. I certainly had a code that I operated by, but I also knew when to play hardball. It wasn't all adorable innocence.

There was another time back when we were with Metromedia when the company decided to breach the agreement we had. The agreement stated Merv would come on at 8:30 p.m.—prime time— and we were doing well in that slot all over the country. You can imagine my surprise when the president of the company at the time, Bob Bennett, called me to deliver the news that we were being bumped from our slot. "You're off the air at 8:30," he said. "You're going on late night. "

"Wait a minute, we have an agreement. You can't just end it," I told him.

"It's ended," he said. With that, he hung up.

When I told Merv, he asked, "What are we going to do? Just take the late-night slot?"

"No. We're gonna get some firepower." I didn't want to reach out to my lawyer, or Merv's old attorney from New York. They were boring. We needed to bring the big guns if we were going to have an impact on Metromedia.

I'd read about Melvin Belli, one of the toughest lawyers out there at the time, with a host of celebrity clients to his name. I knew he was connected to people at William Morris, and I'd always maintained my relationship with the guys there, including Sam Weisbord, a talent agent who became chairman emeritus of the agency, and one of the men to whom I used to deliver mail.

Sam was quite a guy, a health nut during a time when that was quite unusual. He used to work out with a medicine ball every morning. He'd always ask me, "Murray, did you eat your oatmeal today?"

I hated oatmeal—I much preferred coffee and doughnuts from the Schrafft's cart—but I always said, "Of course I did, Sam."

I called Sam to ask if he could get me a meeting with Belli, and he set it up. Belli's office was in San Francisco, and I flew out there to tell him what was happening. It was a beautiful building, an old brownstone with a cast-iron frame and heavy wooden beams inside. The office was almost as imposing as Belli himself. *Oh God*, I thought, *don't let me fuck this up.* I couldn't have done too bad of a job, though, because he agreed to take the case. He flew out with me the next morning.

We met with Metromedia in a big conference room at William Morris, rather than at one of our offices, to keep things on neutral ground. Belli was a sight to be seen, well dressed, with flowing gray hair and a big red pocket silk hanging out of his jacket. He was wearing cowboy boots. When everyone walked in, he leaned back in his chair and put those big cowboy boots up on the desk—I guess he thought they made him look taller, and it really worked. Boy, did he cut a swath. Sam was there too.

The first thing Belli said was, "We're taking you on." Everyone at Metromedia turned white. That's when I took over. I had all the documents with me, and I laid them out and began handling the meeting. We covered what they could do and what they couldn't, and I ended up making a great long-term deal. We settled it all right there. Meanwhile, Belli never dictated anything. I orchestrated the whole conversation—I just used him as my A-bomb.

After the meeting, I went out and bought myself a pair of cowboy boots, just like his. I've always been true to myself, but I'm certainly impressionable in some respects.

Afterward, Belli sent us a bill for $20,000. Merv couldn't believe it. "$20,000?!" he said.

"Merv, do you know how cheap that was?" He didn't realize we'd gotten a great result for what was essentially an extremely low price, given the cost of litigation, bad press, and everything else that could've come from Metromedia's actions.

I was always cautious with dough—when you're running your own company, it's your cash that you're spending, not shareholders'. After all those years of dealing with George, I learned that when you're not sure of how to handle something financial, first consider what you'd do if it were your own cash on the line. I knew when to open my wallet. Melvin Belli was worth it. I still have his books, and I look at them every once in a while when I need help. I usually get better advice from them than I do my own stupid lawyers.

But Merv didn't have to take my word for it. Sam knew how well I'd handled the situation. He was so impressed by it that he wrote a letter to Merv, telling him so:

Dear Merv:

This is a most unusual letter for me to write, and yet I am compelled to do so. Normally, the client praises the agent. In this case, it's the agent extolling the virtues of the client. Your Murray Schwartz and our Murray Schwartz (if you have William Morris blood in you, you have it forever) has shown himself again to be a veritable giant. In his meeting with Bob Bennett, Murray was cool, strong, determined, unflappable, filled to the brim with every conceivable fact and memo, and always made the most exquisite good sense without in any way ever losing his cool. He worked the meeting like a scientist. He pressed along his path like a great military strategist and yet was never unreasoning or unreasonable. He is one hell of a guy in a fight. I tell you with total candor and sheer pride in a former associate, I literally enjoyed the encounter.

I believe a maximum was achieved, but more importantly, Metromedia and you have locked in an affectionate embrace which gives us a clearer road into the future.

My congratulations, and my best to Murray.
Affectionately,
Sam Weisbord

Without me, Merv would never have made a move like that, and it paid off in spades. I looked up to him like an older brother, but in reality, I probably played that role in our relationship. I just had more street smarts than he did.

By the same token, I didn't have the skills Merv had as a performer. Today, people love to tell kids that they can be anything they want to be, but it's just not true. I could never have been a basketball player—I'm just too short—and I wasn't made for the stage the way Merv was. Over the years, I've learned that what you can do is be the best of who you are, and when Merv and I were working together, we were our best selves. We were even better together.

Merv and I really complemented each other. We had a kind of business brotherhood. It went on for many years and brought us far more fulfillment than most business partners experience, in terms of both longevity and success. It could have gone on a lot longer, though.

Merv's jealousy, the daily discomfort of living a lie, eventually broke us. In "Desiderata," Max Ehrmann wrote, "If you compare yourself with others, you may become vain or bitter, for always there will be greater and lesser persons than yourself."[6] How true that is. For many years I've kept that wonderful reading posted in a few places throughout my home, where I'm always sure to see it. I've learned that lessons from all the shrinks, self-help books, and memes out there can all be found in some form in "Desiderata."

We had built this amazing company together that at times employed more than a thousand people, and worked toward dreams we couldn't possibly have fathomed before we met. But ultimately, Merv just couldn't enjoy it—the world wouldn't let him.

It was our societal mores—our strange culture—that kept him from acknowledging who he really was. He thought he'd reached a plateau in his life, where the pain of hiding who he was became too great, and he determined that he wanted, or perhaps needed, something different. But our run wasn't nearly done.

---

6 Max Ehrmann, "Desiderata," 1927.

When Merv started out, he had a great eye for talent. He was smart about the people he put on his show, and those he surrounded himself with. He was smart to choose me, if I do say so myself. We balanced each other out and made a great team.

But because of the times, he couldn't enjoy his life. As a result, I think he felt he had to blow everything up.

Would things have turned out differently if we were operating in today's world, and Merv could've been who he was—able to come out and have boyfriends, even get married and have a kid through surrogacy or adoption if he'd wanted? I think if he'd had the same freedoms I had, things would have been very different.

He could have found someone who liked him for him, instead of a pimp like Brent and the other hangers-on that punished him in the end. Him being with Brent was the equivalent of me picking up a chronic crack addict in Vegas and trying to date her. He could have found someone so much better. He had the opportunity to meet all of these wonderful people, and yet he ended up with lowest of the low.

In those days, though, he didn't have much of a choice—he had to take what he could get. Long after our relationship ended, I was on a flight, and the stranger next to me and I began chatting. He asked what I did and I told him.

"Oh!" the man said. "I know Merv Griffin very well. He just went into business with a dear friend of mine, actually."

"Really? What kind of business?"

"Greeting cards."

The greeting card business? I thought. That didn't sound like something Merv would be interested in.

Then it occurred to me. "You know," I said. "I think I know your friend. Does he look like Tab Hunter?" (I knew Merv had always been attracted to Tab Hunter.)

"Oh my gosh, he looks just like him!" the man said.

I nodded. Merv would have gone into the dog food business for a guy that looked like Tab Hunter.

Had he had the chance to have a real relationship, I think that would've kept him from walking away from what we'd built. He wouldn't have felt compelled to give it away before we reached our pinnacle. We had all of this leverage—shows, the entire block of Hollywood and Vine. Who knew where our company was going? Who knows how many more years we could've gone on for, what we could have accomplished? What would his life have been like? Would he have eaten less and stayed healthier? Would he have lived longer? Woulda, coulda, shoulda, as I always say. But at the same time, it's hard not to long for something that could have been but never was.

I had visions of us developing a studio, of serving as chairman of a huge conglomerate, of Merv and me making more magic together. It was a vision I'd never achieve. Instead, everything we'd done together ended because of Brent's manipulation and Merv's bad judgment.

CHAPTER 15

It Hurts Like Hell
Either Way

Everything was going swimmingly. Merv and I had done so well that the firm we were running was now highly valuable. I was making deals left and right, handling things with the utmost honesty, per usual. Then we got an offer. The industrialist Armand Hammer wanted to buy our company. Merv had met Armand through a tax scheme that involved buying Arabian horses. The concept failed; nevertheless, Merv was impressed by him.

Armand and I had always gotten along wonderfully—I even have a beautiful letter from him praising my leadership. In it, he described his long-term plan to take over the company and have me run it. But Armand was a rough businessman, and I knew the deal wasn't worth our while. He offered to give Merv a million bucks in cash immediately and then buy the company for $69 million—leveraging the earnings. At that sale price, Armand would essentially be stealing the company if Merv agreed to his offer. But the deal was designed

191

to convince Merv it was the right thing to do. He was wowed by the idea of $70 million, caught up in his own importance and how much that number would impress Brent.

I knew Merv Griffin Enterprises was worth far more than that, though I wasn't sure exactly how much. Plus, I just didn't want to sell. I knew we had more ground to cover, that we hadn't yet reached our peak—not even close. But Merv was the chairman, and he overruled me.

I met with Bob Murphy, our executive vice president and Merv's childhood pal, and said, "If Merv's thinking about selling, maybe you and I should buy the company."

"How could we afford to do that?" Bob asked.

"Well, we can get a million dollars—that's easy. Then we can leverage the loan with the income to service the debt." Since I knew what the earnings were, it wouldn't be hard to service the bank's debt.

Bob was a really nice guy and a great drinking buddy. He never took sides in a meeting. We were friendly; I even helped him decorate his office, which was so comfortable that he'd fall asleep in it from time to time. But he did keep a little piece of paper in his wallet where, in the tiniest script I've ever seen, he tabulated how much he was being paid out and how much he anticipated making over the course of the next year, as well as the four that followed. I never knew why he kept that little piece of paper.

He was also close to Merv on a level I wasn't—they'd been friends since they were kids. In high school, Bob had been the popular football player and Merv had been the chubby singer. Of course, since then, their roles had reversed, and Merv was the one making the plays. Bob always projected this image of a fun, understated, easygoing guy. After we sold the company to Coca-Cola, his first purchases were a yellow Rolls-Royce convertible and a new Hollywood wardrobe from Bijan, a boutique on Rodeo Drive considered to be the most expensive men's store in the world (today, their suits go for $25,000 a pop).[1] So much for appearances.

I could have matched what Armand was offering—I could have paid more, even. I would've been able to do $100 million, maybe even $125 million. Plus, I thought working with Bob would appease Merv. I thought by partnering with him, I could show Merv it wasn't just me who wanted the deal—that we were invested in the future of the company and going to make him a fair offer.

But Merv wasn't interested in selling it to me. When Bob broached the subject with him, Merv told him he'd never let me buy Merv Griffin Enterprises. He would've taken the deal from Armand Hammer, but he couldn't envision *Murray Schwartz* owning the company. No amount of money would have been enough.

I heard about what Merv had said and confronted him: "If you'd sell to Armand Hammer, why not me?"

"It's just not a good fit," he said. "I don't even want to discuss it."

I realized that as the company was getting more successful, Merv was concerned that I was becoming far too important. He didn't want me to do well on my own, because then I wouldn't be dependent on him anymore.

At the beginning, everyone had wanted to talk to the star of the show; they didn't want to talk to me. But I'd learned to speak softly in meetings so that they'd lean forward and listen. I was getting

---

1 "Inside the House of Bijan, the Most Expensive Men's Store in the World, Where Suits Go For $25,000," *Inside Edition*, July 31, 2018, https://www.insideedition.com/inside-house-bijan-most-expensive-mens-store-world-where-suits-go-25000-45558.

more powerful, and that was fine for years—I was just covering my territory, while he took care of his.

Eventually, though, Merv began to compete with me. But there was no reason to compete. He was the chairman—the company was called Merv Griffin Enterprises. Still, he started to worry that I'd become the next Abe Lastfogel, the president of William Morris back when I first started out in the mailroom.

A man named William Morris had established the agency, and he had a son, William Morris Jr., who became somewhat of a playboy. Before that, though, he ran things. Meanwhile, Abe Lastfogel lived on the Lower East Side, where the office was originally located. When he was thirteen or fourteen years old, he went looking for a job. He had two options: to work for a tailor at a shop uptown or to become a messenger at William Morris. He chose the latter and worked his way up the ladder until he was the one running things, despite the company name. William Morris Jr. had a small office someplace, but he was never really involved in the business—certainly not the way Abe was; Abe was the one in charge. During his tenure, he maintained the concept that a guy could come from the mailroom, be trained, and move up the ladder.

Merv told Bob about his fear, but I never would have usurped him in that way—it just wasn't my style. I was loyal until the end.

Merv, Bob, and I went to that meeting with Armand Hammer, where he formally presented his offer. It looked as if things were going well for Armand. When the meeting ended, I walked out of the room last, following behind Armand and his lawyer. As they proceeded down the hall, Armand put his arm around his lawyer and I overheard him say, "I told you we'd get it from him."

I told Merv about the exchange. "You're getting taken," I said. He listened to me, and it killed the deal. Hammer despised me after that. So much for that nice letter, huh?

Around that time, my contract was about to expire. I didn't really trust Merv anymore, and I knew that if he sold the company after that contract was up, even if I was still working with him in the same capacity, I would've had a real legal problem on my hands.

I probably would've had a great case, but I didn't want to deal with all that. Besides, the tension between us never quite reached that level. Still, I was concerned about what would happen if our official agreement ran out. I was raking in big percentage payouts, and I wasn't sure if they'd end.

Then, one night, Sol Leon, the senior agent who'd represented Merv with me at William Morris, called and said, "There's a rumor you might be for sale."

"Could be. Sol, you know me. For the right price, my shoes are for sale." Then I said, "I guess I would be for sale to the right company."

"How's Coca-Cola?"

"Yeah, that could be one."

Sol and I had stayed friendly. He was a handsome man whose sophistication was only enhanced by his terrific gray hair. In retrospect, I think having someone more senior to report to at William Morris, a mentor of sorts, was good for me. As much as I felt like I was doing a lot of the legwork, he had more wisdom and experience, and I benefited from that. We don't do that enough in today's society. Age isn't really respected anymore—everyone just wants a newer model. But to me, gray hair means information center.

I always trusted Sol. Remember, when I planned to resign from William Morris to start a company with Merv, he was the first one I told.

When he would come to California, the two of us would have lunch at the Brown Derby on Vine Street—a real piece of Hollywood history. There's a famous story about the director Ernst Lubitsch and the Brown Derby. He was out to dinner there with a star when he told the gal he'd like a blow job. So she did the logical thing: she requested a screen, had it placed around the table, got on her knees, and went to town.

Of course, there were many other arrangements made at the Brown Derby, ones much more appropriate to share in mixed company—they say Clark Gable proposed to Carole Lombard there, for instance—but that Lubitsch tale was a part of its remarkable past too.

Sol and I would meet there, order the Cobb salad, and catch up. He was always very decent, even though I knew he wished he was doing what I was doing. So when he gave me the heads up about Coca-Cola, I trusted him.

The deal was negotiated in New York. The night before the meeting to sell the company, Bob Murphy got so drunk he never showed up to the meeting.

Merv wasn't there either. It was one of the strangest decisions I ever saw him make. You don't go out of the country when you're in the midst of doing the biggest deal of your life. Rather than attending the meeting, he chose to go to Brazil. Later on, he claimed he went to hear some jazz, while his emissaries kept in touch with him regarding the proceedings. But he wasn't there to hear jazz. If he wanted to hear jazz, he would've listened to his Walkman at the time, especially given what was happening in New York.

In reality, he was on vacation with Brent; he was more concerned about impressing him than anything else. Life is not only about conditions; it's about decisions. I continued to wonder about Merv's, and their impact on both of us. In fact, for years after it all ended, I wondered: *If Merv hadn't met Brent while waiting for my plane to arrive from Africa, would we have ever sold the company?* I don't think we would have.

I was stunned by Merv's decision to go to Brazil. I still don't know why he did it, but he left the negotiations entirely up to me. Was it a vote of confidence? Did he have mixed feelings about selling? We spoke on the phone, and he gave me autonomy, saying, "Do what you think is right."

Our lawyer Roy Blakeman and I attended the meeting at the home of Columbia Pictures, which Coke had purchased: 711 Fifth Avenue (it's the one asset they didn't sell to Sony when they decided to get out of the business; the company is still there to this day).

The meeting started at nine in the morning. They offered to pay us $200 million for Merv Griffin Enterprises. "Take it or leave it," they said.

With Merv's go-ahead, I did what I thought was right. "We're not taking the deal," I said.

"Do you know what you just did?" said Roy after the meeting.

"I sure do," I said. "I don't think it's a take-it-or-leave-it deal. I think there's more on the table." They had allowed me to continue talking, ordered lunch from the fancy French restaurant downstairs. If that was it, they wouldn't have let the meeting go on the way it did.

Later that day, Frank Biondi, who was chairman of Coca-Cola Television, called me. "Let's talk," he said.

"I'm leaving for LA today," I told him (I wasn't, but he didn't need to know that).

"Let's have dinner before you go," he said.

We then had a dinner meeting in a private dining room at the 21 Club, where I felt more in my element than in Coca-Cola's elegant boardroom. The ceiling of the main dining room is covered with stuff—old footballs, trains, and more. They're artifacts of industry, representing the big deals that have been made there. A bottle of Coke hangs from the ceiling as well, and I've been told it represents what went down that night.

I used every negotiating skill I had learned to advance the offer from a $200 million "take it or leave it" offer to a $250 million deal with sign-on bonuses, high-paying five-year contracts, cars, the works. How? By getting profit participation. That is, Coca-Cola would reach a threshold of gross profits; after that, we'd get a percentage of the profits in addition to the other benefits I negotiated . . . all while Merv was in Brazil with Brent. In today's dollars, that deal would be over a billion dollars.

In a few short years I'd done what I set out to do and built a major entertainment company poised to go public. When I'd arrived in California, the company consisted of Merv's secretary, a young assistant, and Bob Murphy. By the time we sold, we had five radio stations and a racing patrol service, which taped horse races. We owned Trans American Video—the business I'd bought from Sammy Davis Jr.—and various audio companies, plus the entire block north of Hollywood and Vine and the TAV Theater, a fleet of mobile studios, and soundstages. Honestly, Coca-Cola got a bargain. But in the end, I got the best deal I could have under the circumstances.

Merv's birthday came around shortly after we'd sold the company, and I bought him a gorgeous Ralph Lauren shawl-collar camel hair sweater. While I was in New York on business, he wrote a letter to thank me:

Dear Murray,

Thank you so much for the magnificent Lauren sweater. I'll be wrapped in luxury all fall and winter, and right down to my knees.

What a year it's been so far. Hardly even enough time to lean back and realize what's happened. You must be very proud of what you've accomplished. Very few of us are privileged to realize that kind of accomplishment in their lifetime. Here's to a glorious and happy future wherever this yellow brick road takes us.

Gratefully,
Merv

I thought his reference to the yellow brick road was charming when I first read it. But considering all that happened to us afterward, it seemed to hold a hidden meaning—an elegy for a future that hadn't yet unfolded.

* * *

Life is a choice, and as much as Merv was limited by his sexuality in our era, he had options. But all that frustration—all that ego—that Merv had built up also fueled all kinds of bad moves, including his decision to get involved with a guy named Mike Nigris.

Mike had come into the picture back when Merv and I were still working together. We'd been with the same accounting firm for many years. Eventually our regular guy retired and we inherited Nigris, a young accountant. The firm told us it would be assigning him to us because he could fly out to California to meet with us from time to time.

"Merv," I said, "we've got a new accountant. He's going to fly out here. Do you want to meet him?"

"That's your department," he told me. "You meet with him."

Merv may have spoken with him for a few minutes when he dropped by the office, but that was the extent of the connection they made. I was the one in charge of that relationship. To Merv, it was yet another aspect of the business side, and that was my territory. "I'm bored," he'd often joke during meetings, before getting up and walking away. His boredom with business details was later reflected in his willingness to make decisions without knowing the facts.

I always thought there was something fishy about Nigris. Whenever he came out to LA, presumably to meet with us, he couldn't get it together in the evenings. I would invite him to dinner and he would tell me, "No, no, no—I got other things to do." I'd been around long enough to know that was a problem, particularly when I was supposed to be the reason for his visit.

After we sold the company, Nigris sold Merv a bill of goods. Or maybe Nigris had something on Merv—something he threatened to reveal. Whatever the situation was, their relationship changed. They became close. Merv placed enormous trust in him. And then Nigris conned him.

After the sale to Coca-Cola, Merv decided he would split Merv Griffin Enterprises into two different companies. I would be president of one of them, and he'd make Nigris president, treasurer, and CEO of the other one. On top of that, he gave him a ten-year contract. Merv had never given me more than a five-year contract. For years I worked without an agreement at all, under nothing more than a handshake. Nigris didn't pass my smell test. But no one consulted me about the decision to give him so much power.

For me, that was the final straw. I knew I had to pack it in. It was morally wrong to divvy up what we'd built—a real betrayal. Moreover, Nigris had always been secretive. I knew he wasn't trustworthy.

I resigned from Merv Griffin Enterprises soon after the Coca-Cola deal closed. I stuck around for a few months, just to get everything in order. I'd been there for almost twenty years, after all, and I always remained committed to doing the right thing. Merv was grateful for that. "You're a real gentleman," he told me.

"Thanks," I said.

But I knew Coca-Cola had gotten a bargain, and I fell into a funk. After years of hard work, Merv had ended it all by pulling the rug out from under me—and himself.

I decided to travel for a bit, visiting Moscow and St. Petersburg. I met a lovely German woman during my travels, and we hung out for a while. We had a great time, but I had a lingering sense of sadness, an utter disappointment about all that could've been and wasn't, and that stuck with me.

I was a relatively young guy, and I'd just gotten a lot of dough—more than I'd ever imagined having—but it couldn't make up for the fact that one of the closest relationships I'd ever had in my life had come to an end.

I'd done all right for myself. Coca-Cola set me up with a five-year contract and a production deal, plus a big office on the Columbia lot, a secretary, a driver, and an assistant. It announced its partnership with Murray Schwartz Productions. All was going well until Columbia Pictures, which Coca-Cola had also bought, made two legendary motion picture flops: *Leonard Part 6* and *Ishtar*.

Bill Cosby had written, produced, and starred in *Leonard Part 6*, a spy parody. It was so bad that Cosby himself went on *Larry King*

Live and discouraged audiences from seeing it—not exactly what we'd call promoting the film. It got horrible reviews. In fact, Gene Siskel called it "the year's worst film involving a major star. That's right, it's worse than *Ishtar*."[2] That was saying a lot. *Ishtar* starred Dustin Hoffman and Warren Beatty, who played American songwriters who travel to Morocco for a gig and wind up in a Cold War standoff. The film's costs exceeded its already huge budget, and it was a box-office failure, making it a full-on financial disaster.

After that, Roberto Goizueta, the head of Coca-Cola, told me to join a few others on his private jet to Atlanta. He wanted to tell me some rather disappointing news before it went public. We'd gotten along very well during the sale, and he wanted to do right by me. "Look," he said. "I don't know how to tell you this, but we made a mistake, so we're getting out of show business. For us, this industry is like pouring Coke syrup into the ocean." Eventually, Coca-Cola sold all of its theatrical holdings to Sony, which really got the best bargain. Merv Griffin Enterprises was and still is an oil well. But I got buried.

There was a no-compete clause in my contract, and when Sony took over, they told me I could either stay on with them or go out on my own and effectively end the agreement Coke had offered. I wasn't going to walk away from big money, so I stayed. But then they refused to provide me with a statement of profits—information I needed to know whether I was getting my fair share. My then-lawyer, Richard Ferko, and I met with Sony's cadre of lawyers. Their lead, Mr. Tashman, a slovenly, heavyset fellow, opened. "You do realize you are taking on the entire Sony organization," he said.

---

2 Gene Siskel, "Siskel's Flicks Picks," *Chicago Tribune*, December 23, 1987.

"Yeah, I do realize that," I responded. "And the worst thing that can happen to me is that I won't get your Christmas card this year." Richard choked from laughter when I said that.

They offered me a settlement that would eliminate most of my profits, along with the next year's negotiated salary. "Not a nickel more or less than my deal," I said.

When they refused, we sued them. Merv was subpoenaed as a witness. Before the final hearing, Tashman met me in the hallway with a check. As a result of my suit, I got the percentage to which I was entitled. There was an unintended result too: Merv got a windfall as well.

"I owe you for what you did," Merv told my lawyer. That was nice. It would've been a lot nicer if Merv had paid some of my legal bills.

Over the course of those five years, I had some hits. I created a theatrical show, *Me & Mrs. Jones*, with Lou Rawls. It was based on the catalog music of Gamble and Huff. We had a long run at the renowned Prince Theater in Philly, known to be a stepping stone to Broadway, and broke all the house records. Frank Biondi, who'd moved to Viacom TV, paid a lot of money for a pilot I worked on with Paul Anka. I did a presentation for a talk show with Ivana Trump. But none of those successes came close to anything Merv and I had done together. Meanwhile, Merv would find himself with a full-on failure on his hands.

* * *

Soon after we sold to Coca-Cola, Mike Nigris convinced Merv to get into real estate and buy the Beverly Hilton. Then he used his sway over him to snooker Merv into an extraordinarily terrible deal: going up against Donald Trump to buy Resorts International, a hotel and casino company that had properties in Atlantic City and the Bahamas.

Trump was building the Taj Mahal in Atlantic City. With an estimated $1 billion in construction costs, it was set to be the most expensive building in the world. He was about halfway through the project and needed more cash. His plan was to buy up the public shares of Resorts International, which also owned the Taj Mahal, and leverage them to cover the Taj's construction costs. That's when Merv made his offer to buy the company.

Had it been me, I would have done research on Nigris in the first place. With the hotel-casino deal on the table, I would have flown out to see exactly what I was buying myself. But Merv didn't do any of that. He was never interested in the details; that's why I was such an asset to him. It was also why he got royally screwed in this particular situation.

Nigris ran with a crew of guys just like him—crooks and swindlers who always put their interests first. He and his buddies saw an opportunity. They could convince Merv to bid high on the shares of Resorts International, offering $36 a piece—a full $14 per share higher than Trump was willing to go. Then, with insider knowledge of what was happening with the deal, they would buy up all the available stock and line their pockets in the process.

That was their primary motive. Nigris and Co. paid no mind to whether Resorts International was a good investment or not—and it most definitely was not.

When it came time to do the deal, Merv went up to Trump Tower in New York—a huge mistake. He basically walked into the lion's den dressed as a piece of meat.

Merv called me shortly after he met with Trump. "Murray," he said, "you would have been so impressed. I just made a deal with Trump. It took fifteen minutes."

"That can't be," I said.

"Oh yeah, I just ran circles around him."

"If you did a deal with Trump in fifteen minutes, you got fucked."

"Oh, Murray, that's jealousy talking," Merv said.

"Well," I responded, "good luck."

Financial publications tell us what happened. In addition to purchasing Trump's stock, Merv paid Trump $63.7 million just to cancel the management contract Trump had with Resorts International. He would end up paying Trump more than he could make on the business—something Trump no doubt knew when he agreed to the deal.[3]

Merv paid a fortune for a handful of defunct properties on the verge of bankruptcy, ones that were especially unimpressive compared to the Taj Mahal that Trump was building right near the Atlantic City location, which Trump got to keep control over as part of the negotiations (Merv sold it to him for $261 million, though Resorts International had already invested more than double that in the property). Merv financed the purchase with $325 million worth of junk bonds.[4] It was just dumb, from start to finish.

Soon after, Merv invited me to check out his new purchase. He was paying for it, so I thought, *Why not?*

"What do you think, Murray?" he asked me. The elevators didn't work. When I was playing blackjack, they had to put a bucket on

---

3 Steven Mufson, "The Wheel of Fortune That Went Awry," *Washington Post*, September 17, 1989.

4 James Warren, "Merv Griffin's Deal of Misfortune," *Orlando Sentinel*, June 8, 1990.

the table to catch the water dripping from the ceiling. In truth, I thought it was a disaster.

Worse, the company was $925 million in debt, with $133.5 million due the following year. Resorts International's cash flow totaled a comparatively paltry $60.2 million. And during the first half of the next year, with those debts looming, it brought in a measly $16 million.[5] It was a sinking ship. Even one of his lawyers stated that Merv had been "overly optimistic" about the deal. Between Resorts International's dismal performance and the amount of leverage it took, it was an all-out disaster. But, as his lawyer explained, "Merv couldn't get it in the forefront of his mind that he couldn't own it all."[6]

Merv also failed to realize that Atlantic City is no Vegas. Whereas people were spending an average of four and a half days in Vegas, they stayed in Atlantic City for an average of four to six hours.[7] And while Vegas's tourists viewed gambling losses as part of their vacation costs, Atlantic City's visitors didn't feel the same way. Plus, the regulations were different in New Jersey—much stricter. In 1989, casinos only got to keep 17 percent of what came in via slot machines, which accounted for the vast majority of revenue.[8] It was yet another reason why this particular investment was an utterly terrible choice.

Less than a year after Merv did the deal from the twenty-sixth floor of Trump Tower, overlooking Central Park and Trump's newly acquired Plaza Hotel, Resorts International filed for bankruptcy.

5 Ibid.
6 Steven Mufson, "The Wheel of Fortune That Went Awry," *Washington Post*, September 17, 1989. https://www.washingtonpost.com/archive/business/1989/09/17/the-wheel-of-fortune-that-went-awry/4932433d-c02b-437a-a7dd-46763ebf421e/.
7 Ibid.
8 Ibid.

Merv ran into yet another issue with Resorts International along the way: The New Jersey Casino Control Commission would grant a license for the Atlantic City property only if Merv fired Mike Nigris. Why? Nigris had been involved with organized crime for decades. How ironic that Merv, the same guy who was shocked to meet Jimmy Blue Eyes and Frank Costello at George Wood's funeral, became involved with a guy in organized crime at this stage of his life. It appears Merv was a better judge of character when he was young.

When Merv dropped him, Nigris turned around and sued him for breach of contract and demanded a buyout of that ten-year agreement Merv had granted him.[9] He claimed he'd had a hand in building Merv's business into the cash cow that it was—fake news in its purest form.

Merv's image had remained untarnished for all of the years we worked together, and now, everything had gone awry. When all of this went down, journalists flocked to me, looking for a sound bite on Merv. "What do you think about him?" they asked. I remained silent. There was no reason for me to climb into the gutter with this mess.

Unfortunately, Merv didn't show me the same kindness. *Vanity Fair* published an article on his success. I wasn't interviewed for the piece—I didn't want to be. In it, Merv said he could've done it all without Murray Schwartz, that he had taught me everything I knew.

And then Merv got nervous. He sent me a handwritten note before the article came out to give me the heads-up. He wrote that the journalist had tricked him into saying those things.

I said, "Merv, you're one of the greatest interviewers of all time. Don't tell me some lightweight *Vanity Fair* reporter tricked you. You

9 Frances Ann Burns, "Suit Against Merv Griffin to Proceed," UPI, February 26, 1990.

took aim at me on purpose, and when you did, you shot yourself in the foot." I didn't even have to do anything—the failed Trump deal spoke for itself. Was I a good luck charm during all those years we worked together? Sure. But I was also the brains of the operation when it came to business, and everything that happened after I left proves it.

Years after our business relationship ended, after Merv had bought the hotels and all that, he wrote a memoir, *Merv: Making the Good Life Last*. It could have been titled *Denial*. In it, he distorted facts. He avoided Brent entirely, as well as any of the negatives that had entered his life. There was no mention of me either. It was as if I had never existed.

* * *

Why did things turn out the way they did between Merv and me? Maybe it was the resentment Merv felt toward me; maybe he just didn't know how to let go—so many of us don't. You can end things respectfully. You can be fair and dignified, creating a plan with the other person's position and feelings in mind, and carry it out intentionally and with empathy. You can give them the opportunity to respond in kind, and that ending can be very beautiful in its own way.

If they don't have the capacity to recognize your diplomacy and tact, and it doesn't end as well as it could have, there's nothing to be done. You can rest easy knowing you tried your very best.

But letting go with grace is a unique skill, one that few people have. I like to think I learned it from my father, from watching him look out for me and others at the Red Mill. That's not a lesson many people get. Whether it wasn't a skill Merv had, or whether he was too hurt by the circumstances of his life to put it into play, Merv couldn't exit our relationship gracefully.

At that point, he didn't have the capacity to recognize the loyalty I'd shown him all those years. It didn't end well, and unfortunately, there was nothing to be done about it.

We were each other's trusted, dependable friends, but from what I've witnessed, any business partnership is a marriage of sorts. And just like marriages, some go on and some don't. I always believed we could've continued to share in the results of our tremendous success. But something shifted between us, and when Nigris came along—a con man with few prior accomplishments, at least ones he could talk about—Merv transferred his loyalty to him. We all know how that turned out.

After everything fell apart, we didn't have much contact. We had lunch a couple of times, and Merv made strange comments to fill the silence.

The last time Merv and I saw each other, we met up for lunch at the Beverly Hilton, which he had bought. He didn't care about the business; he just wanted a place where he could be king and everyone would kiss his ass. I still wasn't willing to do that. "Are you still in that dump in Encino?" he asked me.

"Yeah," I told him. "I'm still in the dump in Encino." I still live there today, and I've spent years making it suit my tastes and sensibilities.

Merv went out and bought a hilltop house and never developed the land. Oddly enough, for all the years that I knew him, he never really had a permanent residence. He was always building—something was always under construction. First it was his New York apartment. Then he rented two different houses in Los Angeles, before buying one he decided wasn't good enough. At the end of his life, he lived in a hotel.

Of course, I understand the appeal of living a hotel—it's such a joy. I'd always wanted to experience it, and I did, getting a place at the Carlyle in New York. But I always had a home, a permanent residence with a housekeeper who knew the place inside and out.

Merv's approach was so different than mine, and I found it fascinating. Years later, it occurred to me. I think his transient approach to life speaks volumes: it was an external display of the turmoil he felt inside, of wanting to change who he was. He was never really allowed to partner with someone he cared about. And unlike homes, you can't buy affection and love.

He also lost touch with the things that made him great. While he'd never had great skill when it came to real estate, he'd been brilliant in show business. But that brilliance seemed to dissipate. He put together some silly production company with a few hangers-on. It would seem that he realized he'd made an error selling the company. If he felt he had done all he could with the first one, why create another?

Merv had become a braggart in a strange, somewhat humorous way. He got famous for hanging around in sweat suits, a team of sycophants fawning over him. That new production company he formed never amounted to much. It was him, his nephew, boyfriend, and a few hangers-on, and mostly they just spouted ideas. He launched a game show for kids called *Click,* which focused on a newfangled thing called the internet, but it failed after just two years.

One day he asked if I would give my opinion on his newest project, a life-size game of Monopoly. He was planning to build a giant board on the floor, with cameras overhead filming the action. The concept violated the number-one rule of game shows: that simplicity is key.

To make matters worse, he'd hired a little person to play the role of Rich Uncle Pennybags—complete with mustache and monocle—and run around the board. After a few minutes, I just shook my head and walked out of the room.

Merv followed me. "Why did you leave?" he asked.

"How could you have a little person running around the board like that? You're making a fool of him. You can't do that."

"Oh Murray, you're so sensitive about things," Merv replied.

"Well, that's my opinion," I responded. And with that, I took myself to lunch.

Subsequently, the Monopoly idea went out the window. How could it have worked? But the sycophants thought it was a great idea.

Then his world collapsed when things ended with Brent, and he turned around and sued Merv for $250 million in palimony, followed in short order by Terrio. During the years we were together, he enjoyed a stellar reputation. Sure, there were always rumors, but LA is a rumor mill. After we went our separate ways, however, the rumors stopped being rumors and Merv appeared a fool. He could have continued on that upward trajectory, head of an eponymous corporation. Instead, he held court at the Beverly Hilton, placated by those hangers-on, just overeating. We both learned that lightning rarely strikes twice, though it was a much harsher lesson for Merv.

And, of course, things were never the same between us after I left.

* * *

We were both lucky in that money was never a problem. Merv had millions upon millions between him and his bottom dollar. He had more than enough to paper over the sadness and disappointment he likely felt.

I was able to build and maintain a comfortable life—and what a comfortable life it is. Dora, my housekeeper, comes every day. My home is as charming as could be. I have gardeners that keep the landscaping green and lovely. I pretty much do what I want to do, when I want to do it. I'm a busy guy; I have a social life. I'm happy, at peace with the way I've lived my life, and all that I get to do now because of it. And I'm grateful that I have the funds to enjoy this particular season. All of this is thanks to Merv and our relationship, and I'll always be grateful to him for that. But it took me a while to stop mourning the things that never happened for us.

The Talmud teaches: "Who is rich? He who is happy with what he has." So much of the struggle in life is learning that lesson; it's not an easy one to master. Most of us are always looking for the next thing—we're never happy to rest on our laurels. Merv never was. He could never get enough, especially later on in life, and he tried to quench the constant urge to do and get more with stuff. Properties, land, food, you name it.

He tried to find fulfillment with newer, shinier people and things. He got rid of our lawyer Roy Blakeman eventually, too, and he'd been with Merv since he was a young man, long before Merv met me. Did money distort his sense of loyalty? Was it his life in the closet? It's hard to say.

Merv never did end up coming out. He could have. By the end of his life, times had changed. He could've made a tremendous impact if he'd decided to be honest about who he was. Instead, he maintained that what he did behind closed doors wasn't anybody's business. As Ray Richmond, a talent coordinator for *The Merv Griffin Show* back in the eighties, so eloquently put it, "He certainly didn't owe us an explanation, but maybe he owed it to himself to remove the suffocating veil he'd been forced to hide behind throughout his adult life."[10]

---

10 Ray Richmond, "Merv Griffin Died a Closeted Homosexual," *Reuters/Hollywood Reporter*, August 16, 2007.

* * *

At the end, when Merv was very ill, his son, Tony, prevented anyone from coming to see him at Cedars-Sinai or talk to him on the phone. I wanted to have my chance to say goodbye, though, so I began calling his hospital room at odd hours. Finally I got through.

"Murray, do you believe all those rumors about me?" Merv asked.

I didn't know what to say. I thought that it would be disingenuous to say no, but I didn't want to say yes and hurt him either.

After a pause I said, "Merv, it doesn't matter what I think. It only matters what you think. What do you care what I think?" I think it was a good answer, a kind one. It was an answer I meant.

Before we hung up, he said, "Murray, I love you."

"I love you too, Merv," I replied. It was the last thing I ever said to him. But I did write him a caring letter about all the fun we'd had over the years. I hope he got to read it. When you have something you want to say to someone, don't hesitate. Say it!

There's that old adage that says, "All good things must come to an end." Is it true? I don't know. But it hurts like hell either way.

CHAPTER 16

"The Dense Weave of Life"

And what about George? He never heard about my move to California, and he never knew I'd become the president of Merv Griffin Enterprises. George died in November 1963, right before the assassination of President Kennedy.

When the news came in, I was stunned. I hadn't lost very many people close to me. In that moment, I forgot about all the awful times, and only recalled the fun and adventures. My mind flashed to his funny walk, the baby chickens at Dinty Moore's with the boys, those alligator shoes, our time spent in Vegas. There would never be another George Wood. I cried.

His lifestyle had finally gotten to him, or so it was said at the time. Rumors about the real story behind George's death swirled for years, and those rumors have never quite settled down to land. In one version, he was "fatally injured" at the Camelot Club in New York. There were whispers that he'd been beaten to death over his involvement with a video jukebox machine called Scopitone, a precursor to MTV.

I've never looked into what happened. No good could come of inquiring whether George met his end in a way other than what was reported in the papers. I heard he'd had a heart attack, and that was enough for me. Even then, I had the phone numbers of people who might have been able to tell me more, and they actually might have done so, if only out of respect for the discretion with which I'd handled George's affairs. But I never called. I do know that he died broke. He'd gambled away everything.

It might strike some people as odd that I didn't dig deeper into the story, but the truth is, the why matters more than the how. George died when he did because his lifestyle was unsustainable. He worked very hard, and it was a hard life to live. He may have rested his feet on his desk for long stretches of the day, his alligator shoes catching the reflection of Manhattan's skyscrapers on their buffed tips, but behind that look of uncaring ease lay raging torments. The torments were half his misery—and their expression was the other half.

I would walk by the Frank E. Campbell Funeral Chapel on 81st and Madison, where all the big stars have their funerals—George included—on my way to and from my apartment at the Carlyle. George haunted that small patch of city for me. I thought of him when I went to my favorite lunch place, EATS, on Madison. And every time I walked through the Carlyle's double doors, I remembered visiting its famous Café Carlyle with him to see an act. He loved the high tea there, with its tea sandwiches and tiered plates of cookies.

George left a lasting echo in my psyche. We return to our past constantly, and those formative voices and places await us. I still see the elegance of George in his prime, the way his manner lit up the room, if not the whole of New York City. As I've said, George taught me more than one lesson on what not to do—but it's the lessons on what I *must* do that have stayed with me. I owe George a debt for showing me how to see. Through George, I elevated myself beyond the El on Jerome Avenue. It was George who instilled in me a faith in myself and in my beliefs, because it was George who respected the way I held my own in the tumultuous situations into which he threw me.

And it was the Red Mill that molded me into a person who could stand up to George in the first place. The Red Mill came alive at night, and eventually, so did I. George was custom made for me at that moment in my life. I arrived at William Morris with only a vague idea about getting ahead. George gave shape to that idea.

There's no single cause to our lives or what becomes of them, and no sole event or person lights the fuse that ignites our dreams or snuffs them out. I know it seems that way plenty of times, and so it seemed to me at the start. I now understand the way life's patterns are woven together. I may have been drawn to George initially by his suits, his coats, his shirts and ties—it was a wrapping I was after, a fine covering for the raw stuff of myself that had come tearing out of the Red Mill—but he ultimately taught me that I'm the best judge of how to live, and that I had to trust my own decisions.

Glamour may have lit the way toward something better than the world I grew up in, but it was the pull of my convictions that truly led me onward. What looks like a mere idiosyncrasy—the desire to fill my house with fresh flowers and the pride I take in my appearance—is actually an expression of my determination to continue caring about the fabric of existence.

What we hold onto is worth noticing. I'm not always conscious of the places where George and I intersect, but every now and again,

I see that he's there, under my skin, still guiding some of my movements. George Wood wasn't like me, nor I like him, but we needed each other at that time in both of our lives. He wanted that bet he placed yesterday to pay off today, or the bet he placed today to pay off tomorrow. And so it is with all of us.

Many years after George died, I was having dinner at La Grenouille in New York—a restaurant I've always loved for its gorgeous floral displays. I was seated on the banquette with my date. When I looked to my left, I saw that George's widow, Lois, was seated next to me with her son, Paul. "Oh, Murray," she said. I was now president of Merv Griffin Enterprises, and she was still beautiful and elegant. I sat down and we shared as many George Wood stories as we could in the time we had. I told only the good stories, of course, and there were plenty. Then she said, "He was so mean to you."

There are always three views on life: yours, mine, and the truth. I never experienced George as mean. Difficult, yes. Self-interested too—but never mean. I never got the sense that he was capable of great depth of feeling toward anyone. Everything you do is an outward reflection of your own self-image. If you can't like yourself, how can you truly like anyone else?

* * *

In my life I've suffered deep disappointments and sorrows that at times appeared never ending; we all have. It's easy to feel sorry for yourself at any particular moment in time, but I try to remember that someone always has it worse than me. When someone asks me how I'm feeling, I know they don't really want to know the answer. We're all fighting our own battles, just trying to make it through. Nobody cares that my feet hurt, or that I'm a little more tired than I'd like to be. So I have a standard line: "Better than most, not as good as some."

No matter what your circumstances are, you can find ways to be miserable. Or you can do the opposite. I had to keep going, and so do you. What drives *you* forward? What glimmers of light come to you in the dark?

When George died, he looked old. The hard living had made its mark. He was sixty-three years old. That was an older age in those days than it is now, and George's lifestyle made it older still. Perhaps he'd done what he'd come here to do. Maybe even he knew the road had run out.

Soon after George died, Nat Lefkowitz called me at home to meet him in the office on a Saturday to clean out George's files. When I made the deal with Sid Gathrid, Jerry Zarowitz, and the boys to bring *The Merv Griffin Show* to Caesars, we'd written the primary deal points down on a napkin before I could send a simple letter agreement. During their due diligence before the sale of the company, Coca-Cola's lawyers found the old napkin and asked if there was anything I'd like to remove from the files. I told the lawyers the same thing I told Mr. Lefkowitz years ago: if there's anything we don't want you to see, it won't be in the files. George had taught me well. The napkin remained in my files.

I've achieved more than I could have imagined when I first arrived at William Morris. Of course, those achievements came alongside the disappointments. My marriage, regrettably, did not lead to happiness. A few years before the sale to Coca-Cola, the stress of being a bachelor father, running a large company, and indulging in too many cigarette-and-booze–fueled Vegas nights took their toll, and I had heart bypass surgery.

The apartment I bought at the Carlyle in New York, the place of my boyhood dreams, was sold after it was destroyed by a flood—and further trashed in my heart by a nasty lawsuit. Its beautiful brass doors are still there, however.

My daughter Suzy passed from cancer. Her daughter, my granddaughter Taylor, moved to Texas to be near her father. We don't see each other often, but we stay in touch. Jenny got married, had kids, and got divorced. Like many adult children today, she has decided to become estranged from me. I have two granddaughters with whom I don't have a relationship, and it's an ongoing source of pain in my life.

Dostoevsky said, "To love is to suffer." I think that's pretty extreme, but we all have tragedies in our lives. We all get hurt and offended sometimes. We simply can't control it all—no matter how hard we try. But that doesn't mean we're incapable of shaping our own reality. The question is, how do we live with those experiences, and how do we overcome them?

There's an old Jewish joke about a guy who goes to an art museum with a friend of his. He sees a big white canvas, and in the lower right-hand corner is a little black dot. "What do you think of the piece?" his friend asks.

"You know," the guy responds, "it's a little too much." In contrast, most of us focus on the negative space—all that white canvas. As such, it's easy to notice what's missing, rather than everything else that's there.

In his book *Happiness Is a Serious Problem*, Dennis Prager has a chapter titled "The Missing Tiles." In it, he asks his readers to imagine that they're sitting in a room where one of the tiles is missing from the ceiling. Then he asks what the readers would concentrate on in that room. The answer is the missing tile, of course.

Prager tells us that noticing the missing tile works when we're evaluating ceilings—we can always fix them and make them perfect—but the same isn't true for life. There will always be something missing. And when we focus on that, rather than all we have, we sacrifice our happiness. He aptly calls it "missing tile syndrome."[1]

But we have a choice. We can focus on that missing tile, or we can pay attention to the rest of the ceiling—the intricate detail of it, the beauty of the lighting fixtures, and other positives—and find a lot more happiness and fulfillment in the process. But as much as we try, some missing tiles aren't as easily ignored.

In my life, the missing tile is Jennifer and her children. I wanted to have a relationship with them so much. She made a choice that I never understood. I tried often to communicate with them, but she wouldn't reciprocate.

I'm proud of the devotion that I gave and the sacrifices I made for her and Suzy at a time when being a single father was a curiosity. Many men, especially at that time, wouldn't have taken on the heartfelt responsibilities and challenges of balancing career and parenting. I couldn't be a stay-at-home dad. I had a life too—and I needed a paycheck. My work provided me the means to give them a good life: a warm home, the best schooling—along with love, of course. I chose to give my children everything I could, and I don't regret that choice at all. It didn't work out the way I thought it would. Jennifer's choice is a wound that has never healed, despite the years. Perhaps someday she'll understand there was a better way.

There are a lot of things I miss about running Merv Griffin Enterprises too. I miss the action. To this day, I miss it. All the fun of it, the power. When you have clout in Hollywood, you get invited to all of the good parties, all of the screenings and openings. And when

---

1 Dennis Prager, *Happiness Is a Serious Problem* (New York: Harper Perennial, 1998).

you don't, all of those invitations begin to fade away. That's not just the reality for Murray Schwartz; it's true for everybody in this town.

I don't get invited to the Emmys anymore, though I'd very much like to go again. I loved going out to nice places for lunch with the guys from the office and dressing for the occasion. I miss that too. Who wouldn't?

I still go to those nice lunches sometimes, with friends or on my own with a copy of the *Wall Street Journal*. But when I'm at the Polo Lounge or Spago, I'm not the ex-president of Merv Griffin Enterprises—I'm just a pleasant guy who's nice to people, and that's what's important.

Still, it's hard to know who you are when your life changes. When a heart surgeon retires, he's just a regular guy walking down the street. He loses a big part of his identity, and that's a lot to reconcile.

I was friendly with one of the big names in the business, a guy I'd delivered mail to in the old days. One time, over lunch at The Grill in Beverly Hills, he asked me what my net worth was.

We were both getting older; I was no longer the kid delivering his mail, but I was still taken aback by his question. Who asks someone something like that? Plus, it's so hard to derive the truth. A quick Google search will tell you how much property a guy has and what it's worth, but it won't tell you that $9.5 million of that beautiful $10 million house he's got is mortgaged. It's just another way people keep score, but it doesn't really mean anything.

Joe E. Lewis once said, "I've been rich and I've been poor. Rich is better!" While it's a funny line, it's not true. Remember, if you're happy, then you're a happy guy with money. If you're miserable, that money won't do a damn thing for your state of mind. For that reason,

I've never lived an excessive lifestyle. I have one car, not three or four. In my experience, those who are excessive aren't happy. A dear buddy of mine had ten cars when he died. How much money did he leave behind? All of it.

When my companion asked me my net worth, I responded, "Gee, I don't even know, I never discuss things like that."

"Are you worth more than me?" he asked.

"Maybe, maybe not."

He paused for a second and then asked, "How do you stay happy?"

"What do you mean 'how do you stay happy?'"

"Without my work, I feel like I'm nobody, like I'm nothing." What a life lesson that was. Most of us don't know who we are without those external indicators of worth. That's because many of us lack purpose—something far greater than a fancy title, a snappy car, or dough in the bank. Without a sense of purpose, ethics, values—an internal compass—it's easy to find yourself adrift.

* * *

Every family is plagued with its own issues, but I had an advantage. We may not have had much growing up, but I knew who I was. My father had bestowed upon me a number of gifts—some more illicit than others—but a sense of self was among the most powerful ones I got. I took it with me wherever I went, and it allowed me to belong wherever I found myself—from the strip club to Spago.

I think it was that gift that kept me from walking away when George told me I dressed like a clown that night at Elmo's. I look back at that young man and can't help but think, *What a pair of goolies on that kid.* But I knew who I was, and because of that, I was able to move forward. That's a skill worth honing—a gift you can give yourself.

223

In the moment, I was offended and embarrassed—of course I was. My feelings were hurt. I could've sought retribution in the form of an HR complaint or simply given up altogether and accepted my place in the mailroom for the foreseeable future. But I didn't do either of those things. I saw an opportunity when it came my way, in the form of that glowing Bond Clothiers sign in Times Square, and I took it. I bought that blue suit and went back to El Morocco.

When suddenly you seem to lose all you thought you had gained, do not despair. You must expect setbacks and regressions. Don't say to yourself "All is lost. I have to start all over again." This is not true. What you have gained...When you return to the road, you return to the place where you left it, not to where you started.

—Henri J.M. Nouwen, *The Inner Voice of Love*

CPSIA information can be obtained
at www.ICGtesting.com
Printed in the USA
LVHW110513050820
662302LV00004B/91/J